PRAYER

PRAYER
A Spiritual Warrior's Guide
To Life's Challenges

Tom Virden

First Printing June 2022

Layout and Design: Gary Lebeck

Cover Design: Gary Lebeck

Editor: TJ Martini

Cover Photograph: Olga Yastremska © 2021

Photograph of Tom Virden: Virden Family

Published by Rivertree Media
Reno, Nevada

Printed in the United States of America
26 25 24 23 22/RM/10 9 8 7 6 5 4 3 2 1

Library of Congress Cataloging-in-Publication Data

Names: Virden, Tom, 1954- author. | Martini, TJ, 1948- editor.
Title: Prayer : a spiritual warrior's guide to life's challenges / Tom
   Virden.
Description: First edition. | Reno, Nevada : Rivertree Media, 2022.
Identifiers: LCCN 2022012863 (print) | LCCN 2022012864 (ebook) | ISBN
   9780578393278 (paperback) | ISBN 9780578393278 (kindle edition)
Subjects: LCSH: Prayer--Christianity.
Classification: LCC BV210.3 .V57 2022 (print) | LCC BV210.3 (ebook) | DDC
   248.3/2--dc23/eng/20220407
LC record available at https://lccn.loc.gov/2022012863
LC ebook record available at https://lccn.loc.gov/2022012864

Dedication

This book is lovingly dedicated to my Arabic grandmother, Sitti Della Debbas. Sitti means Grandmother in Arabic, and my Sitti is woven throughout the pages of this book. During her life, she exemplified the true spirit of Christ better than anyone I have ever met. When I was young, she showed me and my brothers more love and spiritual guidance than any other person in my life. Despite my turning from God at a young age, it was the foundation she modeled that never left me, even as I wondered on the dark side for more than 13 years. Thank you, Sitti Della from the bottom of my heart. I can't wait to see your beautiful, loving eyes again in Heaven someday.

Table of Contents

Acknowledgements

I want to thank everyone who has touched my life throughout this project even if you were not mentioned in this book. You made a difference, and I am so grateful. That being said, I am going to try and call out several wonderful people who had such a significant impact on me that I cannot help but give them the credit they deserve in shaping me as a man and Christ follower. For several years, I resisted starting this project, but when God sent me to a place called Winnemucca, Nevada, to live and work, I finally gave in and began to write. I felt like Jonah being spit out on a foreign beach, where I knew no one, and I literally had nothing to do but work.

While in Reno, I led a community group at South Reno Living Stones Church for five years and my usual prayer requests from them was that I start to obey God and start writing again. One of the precious women in the group was Kathy McAlpine. She constantly encouraged me to write, and she even bought me two books on the subject for my going away party. Right after my move to Winnemucca, I read them both in two nights, and in my Nineveh-sparked moment, I felt a longing to do what God had been prompting me to do for so long. So, thank you Kathy for your prompting, and thank you to all my community group "The Wild Bunch" for all your prayers and support.

I thank my Pastor Ryan Griffin of South Reno Living Stones Church who took me under his wings at a time of complete weakness in my life after my divorce. He is a true spiritual warrior and, despite my brokenness, he saw in me the potential of leadership. With his caring guidance and spiritual strength, Ryan picked me up, dusted me off, and got me back in the game! So, thank you Pastor Ryan for being such a great friend and an awesome spiritual coach.

I also want to thank all the men who came week after week to the men's prayer group who all the lessons in this book were created for. Men like Amos Womble, Bob Turner, my nephew Tyler Virden, who is now with the Lord, Garret Bebe, John Miller, John Hughes, Joe Skrechko, Steve Blankenbush, and Travis Echevarria.

These books below are the ones that helped me formulate my views and outlook on prayer over the years. I am so grateful for them all.

1. Beautiful Outlaw by Joihn Eldridge

2. Moving Mountains by John Eldridge

3. Armed and dangerous by John Ramirez

4. The Prayer Ministry of the Church by Watchman Nee

5. Experiencing God Day by Day by Henry T Blackaby and Richard Blackaby

As I sit here writing this, I also see countless faces that came and went as the years went by. I see tough men whose faces were dripping tears as they prayed for each other; I see them struggling to find Bible verses and mis-reading Scripture as it was no doubt the first time that they ever held a Bible in their hands. This book is truly dedicated to them, as they made it possible with a crazy desire to meet up with some old car salesman and open their hearts up to each other. Thank you, men!

I thank Jerry Barringer who is a true spiritual warrior and man of prayer. Jerry is someone I met as a young Christian who has been through ten thousand phone calls giving me a spiritual uplifting and biblical perspective through the many challenges that I have faced over 40 years at this walk. His kind nature and ever caring heart is the purest example of a Christ follower. He is a true brother in Christ.

I want to thank all my enemies I have battled in 50 years of the car business, both men and women who were bent on my destruction. They all gave me the opportunity to show God's love and power over any situation and helped me learn to rely on Jesus when all else failed. They collectively watched in amazement as I trusted God instead of retaliating and in the end, most were amazed at the outcome.

I have to thank my five children who have inspired me to

always be the best man I could ever be. Despite my many failures over the years, none of them has ever turned their back on me and all of them give me a joy beyond description. So, thank you Tommy, Kacie, Danny, Cody and my little mini me Alese. You are all truly my heart's delight.

And most of all, I want to thank my Lord and Savior Jesus Christ, for His guidance and direction, and His nudges throughout this entire project. For without Him, this would not have been. Thank You, Lord, for loving me, and for forgiving me for all the poor choices I've made throughout my life and protecting me from them all. Thank You, too, for never giving up on me. You are my Rock, my Hero, my Friend, and my Savior. You the reason I am alive today and I cannot thank You enough!

Foreword

BY HOMER STEVENS

I am Apache; born into a Christian family. My family is from a small reservation town in Arizona where servitude to God and family are ideals. I served as an altar boy within my Church until I was 15. Within my family, I continue to try to live the best Christian life possible.

I met Tom Virden in 1988, when he came to Arizona for a bear hunt. I am a hunting guide. Tom was referred to me by another hunter. As we began our hunt, Tom and I got to talking a little and I began to feel comfortable with him. As our conversations stretched on during that initial evening, I decided to stay around longer with Tom beyond our hunt. Through our conversations I found out we had a lot in common. This conversation in the wilderness began the foundation of our lifelong friendship.

Out of our conversation and friendship, Tom asked me to be his best man at his wedding a few years later. We grew closer in each other's lives and family. We also continued to hunt together, and our conversations and friendship continued to grow. Soon our friendship grew strong enough to even include a couple of business ventures. Anyways, this is to say by any measurement, we got closer. Through all this growth, Tom and I continued talking about what initially drew us close; it was our faith and our families.

"Count it all joy, my brothers, when you meet trials of various kinds, for you know that the testing of your faith produces steadfastness." **(James 1:2-3)**

I helped Tom through his hard times. We helped moved his family a few times due to employment opportunities. As you know, this is tough. It becomes tougher when marriages become strained. After twenty some years of marriage, Tom was tested with a divorce. But God provided faith and friendship.

During this trying time, I asked Tom to come to Arizona and live with my family. When I get involved in anything, I'm all in. His problems is my problems. I wanted Tom to be able to clear his mind, and to help him figure what the next right move would be. When Tom came, he also brought his son Danny, and together, we worked through this difficult time.

"So He Himself often withdrew into the wilderness and prayed." **(Luke 5:16)**

While he was with us, Tom helped me with various tasks. We often spent time in the mountains. We prayed about our situation.

During these times we continued our conversations. We took heart understanding that Jesus would also seek out the wilderness in trying times. I can understand. Within my own family, the mountains and the wilderness are an important background to the work of God. It was during these times that a course of action was made apparent to us. After a while Tom decided to go back to Nevada. He was making a new start. I was happy.

"I will praise thee, O Lord, with my whole heart; I will shew forth all thy marvelous works." **(Psalm 9:1)**

Our conversations continued. Sometimes I would go visit Tom or he would come visit me. There were times when our conversations were through phone calls. During one of our visits, Tom told me he had been writing a journal. He said he had been writing for awhile and thought it was time to turn it into a book. I thought it was a great idea. When I started reading some of the script, it caught me off guard and turned out to be an awesome idea.

Being a Christian all my life, I have tried living the best life for God, which I thought I was doing. However, after reading Tom's book, I saw where I was lacking. During our friendship I thought I was helping Tom. I realized that Tom had been documenting a better path with God, not only for himself, but for me and for others.

"Trust in the Lord with all thine heart; and lean not unto thine own understanding." **(Proverb 3:5)**

The biggest change I would make in my life was as to learn to abide with God. Everything I was doing by trying to be good, I was doing for me. I felt I was making points for **me**, for when I messed up in life. I felt like I could use all the good I was doing, or thought I was doing, to help me smooth things over with God. After reading Tom's book, "Prayer: A Spiritual Warrior's Guide to Life's Challenges" I saw that God doesn't keep score. You are either good or you are not. It's up to you and you, and you alone.

"A Prayer Warrior's Guide" is a must read. It will open your heart to God. Thank you, Tom, for helping me see more and understand more so that I am able to come closer to our Father in Heaven and abide with Him.

Amen, my brother. Your friend Homer.

BY JERRY BARRINGER

Among God's greatest gifts during one's lifetime are lasting and inspiring friendships. For me, no friendship has been more fulfilling, or more purposeful or meaningful than with Tom Virden.

In the Gospel of **John 10:10,** Jesus says that, *"I have come that you may have life and have it to the full."* Well, I can say, without hesitation, that Tom Virden has lived his life to the fullest!

You are about to embark on a literary journey that you will discover to be compelling, challenging, and possibly life changing. In a manner unlike any other, Tom combines his amazing life experiences with an emphasis on the power of prayer to demonstrate God's incredible faithfulness and love.

You will be moved by Tom's reflections on how, when, and where God was at work in his life.

I highly recommend this powerful and personal book! I am confident that you will benefit by gaining a deeper understanding of God's Gift of Prayer... It's power, it's purpose and it's promise!

Introduction

The book you're holding, "Prayer: A Spiritual Warrior's Guide to Life's Challenges" was inspired from five years of teaching prayer and how it relates to life's hardships and was taught to mostly unchurched men. The pages inside will take you through many interesting subjects and will entertain you with great stories. The writings will touch your heart and strengthen your resolve to keep moving forward, with an eye to the day when we will all look Jesus in the face and hopefully believe we have done our very best as a person of love.

Whether you believe it or not, inside each one of us is a spiritual warrior waiting to be fully used by God to further His Kingdom, and this book will help you learn to lean hard into your relationship to Jesus through common sense thinking and constant prayer.

The foundation has been laid out for anyone to get through hard times in life's many day-to-day challenges and failures through the power of prayer and backs it up with both raw experience and biblical truth.

Prayer could possibly be the most misunderstood facet of life. This isn't just a Christian problem because everyone prays... even an atheist! We all know that we cannot control our world and we entreat a litany of things to change the things we cannot control. Some ask for luck, some think its karma, some even try to do good in hopes it comes back to them, and the doubting Christians begs God on a regular basis for the things they want to happen in this crazy venture called life.

Sometimes it works and you think you got lucky. Sometimes just the right result happens, and you think your universal energy is balanced and your good fortune is the result. But then again, sometimes it all goes bad, and you start blaming everything and everyone in your life for the hardships that have fallen on you.

Prayer does not mean the same thing to all of us. To Christians, it means a much more serious thing because they are supposed to have a direct connection to the One True God who created and controls the entire universe. So, why do so many Christians miss the mark in their prayer life? Why do they wait till disaster hits to fall on their knees and try to get the supernatural fix to their problems? Why do the faithless people run to God when all else fails ... i.e., no atheists in a fox hole syndrome?

My own father told me of a story about when he was in combat in Korea. One dark and freezing night he had dug himself deep down into a foxhole. As he listened to the gongs and horns of the Chinese army maneuvering around him and his men, in the complete moonless black night and, outnumbered by hundreds, he was scared. So scared, in fact, that he begged God to protect him. My dad even made a deal with God. He promised Him that if he survived the night, he would believe that God was real and would dedicate his life to Him.

The battle started and lasted well into dawn. My dad fought through the night with his carbine and eventually ran out of ammo, at which time it became a hand-to-hand battle with pistols and bayonets. He survived and as the sun started to rise, he described the gruesome scene. Everywhere he looked, there were Chinese soldiers piled up 10 feet high as far out as you could see. His platoon had taken over 50% causalities in that battle as well. Many brave lives on both sides were lost that night, but somehow my father survived and was basically unhurt.

From that day on, my father believed in God, but 70 years later, on his death bed, he cried to me that his life from that point on did not live up to the promise he had made to God so many years before. He did not dedicate his life to God as he had promised, and he wished he would have done more. Sadly, he knew it was too late and his time on earth was coming rapidly to an end.

I tried to console him by pointing out the obvious fact that he had been, for the most part, a great dad and good grandfather, and that God forgives all if we admit our shortcomings and ask for forgiveness. **1 John 1:9** *"But if we confess our sins to him, he is faithful and just to forgive us our sins and to cleanse us from all wickedness."*

My father passed within a few days and the conversation has stayed in my mind since then. I venture my dad is like most of us... we pray when trouble comes, and then when things improve, we get right back to controlling our world and doing whatever it is that makes us happy.

Do you ever wonder why God makes it so hard on us? Why can't we just hear Him clearly when He answers us? Why doesn't He just let us see Him in real time so we could believe without a doubt? Why do we have to beg Him for help? Why do we have to get all the way off the deep end before we seek His help? Why do we have to ask and ask and not know for sure if He is listening? After all, if there are seven billion people in the world and maybe half are Christians, doesn't He have a lot to do listening to three billion people begging for help, and selectively helping some but not others? Who is filtering all that chatter and crying for Him?

Though it doesn't come from the Bible, we have all heard the phase, "God helps those who help themselves." If we were to believe this, maybe we should just forget prayer and go figure it out! God has way too much to do to care about my problems, right? Then you have the people who pray and pray and in the back of their minds don't really believe God is going to answer anyway. Are they right? Are they just wasting time betting on the come line hoping that God will let their dice flip to a seven? And how about those who ask God for a sign, and then when lightning doesn't strike next to them, they say, "See?"

Do you find yourself asking these and other valid questions that make you wonder if the effort of prayer is even worth it, and eventually giving up on prayer itself? I believe most Christians and probably all non-Christians fall into this endless circle of doubt.

As we read through these chapters, we are going to examine all these questions to see if we can't find the proper prayer life and give up trying to have a meaningful prayer life until the next major life shattering event happens. Then it's "let's make a deal" time again, just like my dad!

CHAPTER ONE

What is a Spiritual Warrior?

My hope in writing this book is to encourage you to see yourself as God sees you... a Spiritual Warrior waiting to be used in His grand scheme of sharing His love and saving grace to your family, friends, and even complete strangers!

Are you a Spiritual Warrior? What do you picture in your mind when you think "Spiritual Warrior"?

Is it someone who is wielding a sword like Michael the Arch Angel or a street preacher sneaking through enemy neighborhoods with a Bible and a Glock WORKING AGAINST SATAN and his army of demons?

We are taking a deep dive into prayer here in this book and how it relates to a lot of our life's problems.

The $54,000 question here is, are you enlisted? Maybe you don't think of yourself as a Spiritual Warrior. After all, Spiritual Warriors really are the Pastors, Evangelists, and Missionaries who are all in on the front line of this Spiritual war.

If you do your homework on our US Army you will find that we have about 485,000 soldiers. Only 15% of them or approximately 72,000 are Infantry. Infantry is the boots on the ground weapon-carrying gunfighters of our Army. That leaves 410,000 plus people who are needed to support the front-line warriors. However, they are **all** considered Army. They all deploy in every conceivable capacity to enable the gunfighters to do their jobs!

My point here is that maybe you're a greeter at church, or the person who serves communion. Maybe you're a set-up team member, or a worship team member, or a financial helper, or a deacon or elder behind the scenes? The fact is, you are **all** in "the Service "for the most important war in history... that of the future souls of men and women for eternity and not territory.

In the Army, the gunfighters poke fun at the support people and call them POG's. An acronym for POG is, "Personnel Other than Grunts", though I have never heard in 40 years of serving any front-line troops make fun of their support teams in the church. I have never spoken or heard a word against the POGs in God's Army in the 40 years I have been a front-line gun fighter. God hand picks the team, in our case all of us know when the Holy Spirit talks to us in that powerful, silent-thought, voice prompting, and as always, we have a choice to obey or not.

True meaningful prayer happens when we submit our desires

to do His will in real time. He is calling all of us to enlist and seek our purpose in this war for souls. The gun fighters can't operate alone, unsupported. The enemy knows this and is constantly trying to cut off supply lines and support crews. So, from that perspective we are all Spiritual Warriors!

This book is how we connect the dots, how we function day to day doing His will and following our orders from the ultimate Commander and Chief, Jesus. Learning to dedicate our prayer life through tough times gives us true purpose; it keeps us fighting and working hard with a future-focused laser determination. It is the key to how we earn our metal!

It is how we serve with a glad heart because in the end when your hitch is done, no matter how you served, you will have earned the honor of being called a Veteran. The day will come when you look over a sea of souls in Heaven and you will know that you had a hand in many of them being there!

Maybe you are on the sidelines not wanting to get involved as it might upset your time off or family. Maybe you are afraid to get involved because you think, "How could God need my help?" Truth is, He doesn't, but that doesn't excuse you from the calling.

The draft dodgers in the Viet Nam war ran in shame and fear to other countries or jail instead of serving. I get that maybe many of them had legitimate conscious objections, but they paid the price for their beliefs. We are talking about a war where there is no long-term downside because we are saving people from certain death instead of sending them to early graves. How does the C.O. defense stack up here? It doesn't! Only you can answer the question of whether or not you are side-stepping God's calling. Remember, God looks at the heart, and it's impossible to lie to Him. So, stop fighting against Him and enlist, become the Spiritual Warrior He is calling you to be. And before you start fighting in this battle, be sure you are fully dressed in the Armor of God.

Ephesians 6:10-18: *"Finally, be strong in the Lord and in his mighty power. Put on the full armor of God, so that you can take your stand against the devil's schemes. For our struggle is not against flesh and blood, but against the rulers, against the authorities, against the powers of this dark world and against the spiritual forces of evil in the heavenly realms. Therefore, put on the full armor of God, so that when the day of evil comes, you may be able to stand your ground, and after you have done everything, to stand. Stand firm then, with the belt of truth buckled around your waist, with the breastplate of righteousness in place, and with your feet fitted with the readiness that comes from the gospel of peace. In addition to all this, take up the shield of faith, with which you can extinguish all the flaming arrows of the evil one. Take the helmet of salvation and the sword of the Spirit, which is the word of God. And pray in the Spirit on all occasions with all kinds of prayers and requests. With this in mind, be alert and always keep on praying for all the Lord's people."*

LET'S PRAY...

Dear Jesus, our true Commander and Chief, please cause us to realize how very important we all are to the war You have called us to in the souls of humanity. What an honor to serve such a righteous cause. Give us a raw dose of courage, strengthen our resolve to serve with pure hearts, unselfish motives and to love our worthy enemies. Thank You, Lord that You recruit us, You train us, You discipline us when necessary and You launch us into battle, but never alone. You are with our every step in the front as the point man. You are in command and all we need to do is obey. The victory is guaranteed! Our service is truly a heart thing! Protect us as we serve, in Your Son's precious and Holy name, Jesus Christ. **AMEN**

CHAPTER TWO

Prayer Defined

So, what exactly is prayer? Prayer, simply put, is personal communication with God. So, first I am going to deal with us Christians. We believe that God created all things, including us, and that our Creator wants a relationship with us, or why else would He send His Son down here to take on humanity and die for all of us so that we may become heirs to His kingdom? It doesn't make sense that God would put all this in motion and then say, "I don't want to talk to them now, so let's let randomness take over and see how they do on their own?"

Part of the real issue with us is that God gave us free will to choose. Why would He do that? Well, for one reason, He didn't want to create a race of robots who are programmed to all act alike and always do the right thing. So, instead, He gave us choices. He gave us a brain that could think and make decisions, and a heart that could feel everything, as well as all the results of the choices we make. He gave us a world to live in and other imperfect people around us to relate to, or to hate, or to love on. And most of all, He gave us His Son to redeem us. So why then would He cut us off from talking to Him?

We all have a desire to know God that is innate. It's part of that God-size black hole inside us that can never be satisfied with the things of this world. Our ability to seek God is a choice for sure. You can decide not to and call all Christians weak, but deep down inside there looms the question, "What's really wrong with me?" "Why do I feel like I'm never satisfied?"

When you accept Christ, you are given the Holy Spirit as a gift to unlock the mysteries of God and His creation, and how you should relate to Him if you are making the right choices. Prayer is how you communicate on a personal level, and God loves it when we seek a relationship with Him.

Don't ask me how He does it, but I assure you, He is so far beyond human understanding that we will never get it until we see Him face to face. This is where faith comes in. Science knows it cannot prove there is a God so they deny Him and look for experiments that will prove the theories of how things work. Christians take a much simpler route in choosing to believe that God exists, and that He created us and desires a relationship.

When you get to the core of prayer, you must ask yourself, "Why do we pray?" We pray for three basic reasons:

1. It expresses our trust in God.

2. It brings us to a rich relationship with Him where we learn to trust Him in ALL things.

3. It allows us to be involved in activities that have eternal meaning and gives us a greater purpose in this crazy world we live in!

So how are the ways God can answer our prayers since no prayer goes unheard by this incredible Supreme Being that loves us and cares for us? He could hear your prayer and say, "YES!" **(1 John 5-14-15).** The Bible, which is the living Word of God to us Christians and in this dispensation, says in those verses, *"and this is the confidence that we have before him, that if we ask anything according to his will, he hears us and if we know that he hears us in whatever we ask we know that we have the requests which we have asked from him."* The key here is asking for things in **His** will, not ours!

Another way He answers us is, "I have a better idea for you." In **1 Corinthians 12:9-10**, it tells us that, at times, God's grace **must** be sufficient for us and that His power and our ability to trust Him is perfected in our weakness. Also, when we pray, He may be expecting us to accept the fact that He is going to show us a better way eventually, and we should trust Him because He knows the future. Like in the song from Garth Brooks, "Thank God for Unanswered Prayers." You might not see it now, but eventually the scales will be removed from your eyes, and you will get why certain things you so desperately prayed for are withheld from you, so a much greater blessing might occur in your life, and because granting us a certain request would have derailed God's greater purpose.

When I went through my second divorce after a 25-year relationship, I begged God for three years not to let this happen. My whole self-worth and identity were wrapped up in being a good provider as a hard-working husband and a loyal father to my five kids. My wife wanted out, but I could not let go! God tried to show me that it would be okay and that He had other plans, but I was relentless! Eventually I succumbed to God's answer and turned my hurt over to Him. That's when He began to use me in different ways that I didn't see coming.

God slowly healed my brokenness by getting me involved with other great Christian men like Pastor Ryan Griffin, who invited me to a community group. I took my youngest daughter, who was 13 at the time and was missing her mother, which led me to lead my own community group. I also started a men's prayer group which led to me writing this book.

One night my den was full of both non-Christian and Christian men all seeking a deeper relationship with God. As I shared the Scriptures with them, it dawned on me that had I still been married to the love of my life, our group would not be meeting. God also would not be reaching out to a bunch of lost, wild car salesmen because I would have never seen the need that God had put in my path. The calling He had for me was a much bigger idea than I had, even though I had to suffer in order to see it. Suffering in unanswered prayer should bring us closer to Him, not farther away.

Another way He can answer our prayers is, "Not yet!" **Galatians 4:4** tells us that, *"When the set time had fully come, God* *sent His Son born of a woman, born under the law."* In other words, things happen in God's time, not ours! So, "Not yet" is also an answer to prayer because God already has His plan formed. And by making the right choice to trust His timing when He deems it, that, in time, He will answer your prayer.

There are two important conditions to have a good shot that God is going to answer your prayers. If these two conditions match up to your prayer, let's say your odds are much greater. The first one is, are you abiding in Him? Are you? What does that mean? To abide in something is like living in a house. You abide at this place. In the case of God, are you living your life with Him or are you just stopping in now and then for a coffee like a friendly neighbor to sit and share your problems?

Abiding in Him means that you live with Him day and night. **John 15:7** says, *"If you abide in me and my words abide in you, ask whatever you wish, and it shall be done for you."* So, I'll ask again. Are you abiding in Him? Are His words living in you? If you think that your prayer requests are a big wish list you come to Him with once in a while, when things get bad and you might open up your Bible app occasionally to check a verse, I doubt if this qualifies as abiding in Him... and hence, you are missing a big qualifier!

The other big qualifier is seen in **1 John 5:14-15,** *"And in this confidence which we have before him, that if we ask anything according to his will, he hears us, and if we know that he hears us in whatever we ask we know that we have the requests which we have asked from him."* If you really digest this verse, you have to see that it is not necessarily what we want, but that what we want would align with His will.

So, are the things you so desperately seek from Him something that He so desperately seeks from you? His will? Ironically, how do you figure that out? Obviously it's by praying about it and searching your heart. Actively abiding with him, daily reading His word, and making a white heat, burning effort to surrender your will to His plan for your life here on earth.

So, we looked at two important principles that must be taken seriously, but what else do we do that can knock our prayer requests off the tracks? Asking for things according to our own passions. **James 4:3-4** says, *"You ask and do not receive because you ask with the wrong motives, so that you may spend it on your pleasure. You adulteresses! Do you not know that friendship with the world is hostility toward God? Therefore, whoever wishes to be a friend of the world makes himself an enemy of God."*

Wow, how guilty are we of this today? Every advertising message pounds us with how to be cool so the world around us thinks we are special. We put our faith in the things of the world and wrongly the people of the world who are, for the most part, not abiding in God! And in doing so we willingly self-mutilate our prayers. When you come before God with your prayers and the rest of your life is chasing the job, your hobbies, your family, your kids, or anything else that you chase after, **remember this verse,** and count yourself as an enemy of God!

Be honest... the basis for this is sin! Sin is anything we do wrong in the sight of God—any word, any thought, any action we do against God is sin, and unconfessed sin will also keep God from taking our wish list serious! God has laws that He puts into place and then give us His guard rails so that we don't spin off the road and wind up in a ditch of sin. It is also impossible to live the human life without sin in our thoughts, words, and deeds. If we continue in unrepented, habitual sin, or if we continue to sugar coat our evil hearts, we are taking huge steps in hindering our prayers.

Proverbs 28:9 says, *"He who turns away his ear from listening to the law, even his prayers are an abomination."* Again, does this mean you must live a perfect life to have your prayers heard? Of course not. We're always going to blow it! However, **1 John 1:9** says, *"If we confess our sins, he is faithful and righteous to forgive us our sins and to cleanse us from all unrighteousness."*

Bingo! You have the solution to the sin problem… Confession! However, if you are continually falling into the same sin over and over again, go back and read this again. Are you: Abiding in Him? Reading your Bible daily? Asking for His will, not yours? I believe if you are actively seeking Him, you will be making day-by-day progress.

Maybe you have a problem with pornography… a sexual addiction, and you can't stop. But if you and Jesus were roommates, and He lived and slept in the bedroom next to you, do you think that might stop you from going there in your sneaky little world? Let's say you're eating breakfast with Jesus in the morning, and He says, "Hey, how are you? How is your sin life? Is there anything I can help you with?" You always have choices! You can say, "No, Bro, I'm good." Or you can be honest, and say,

"Yes, Jesus, I'm struggling with a sexual addiction. I can't stop watching porn. I need help with this." And Jesus, being super cool and wanting your life to align with His, says, "Ok, let's pray about this and then read some scriptures that you should memorize to help you gain strength in this area. Because you're not the only person suffering from this! And when we're done, I'm going to use you to help others!" Do you think that prayer secession with Jesus would align up with God's will for your life?

Beating addictions long term is only done with the help of the Holy Spirit! He might say, "I'm also going to put faithful men around you to keep you accountable." **Proverbs 27:17,** *"Iron sharpens iron, so one person sharpens another."*

What about liars and the father of lies—Satan! And his ability to create doubt in our prayer life when we aren't paying attention. Look at **Proverbs 19:22-23,** *"What is desirable in a man is his kindness and loyalty, it is better to be a poor man than a liar, the fear of the Lord leads to life, so that one may sleep satisfied, untouched by evil."* You can lie to everyone around you. You can even lie to yourself. But you cannot lie to God. He knows your heart!

Why do you doubt God will answer when you go to Him in prayer? If you don't think He will, then why bother to pray? That doubt you are feeling comes from Satan, and he is a liar. He wants you to believe that God won't answer you. Do you ever find yourself wondering if God even cares about you? Or that God is just too far away to hear your problems? Or maybe you think that God has way more important things to do, especially these days with the world being upside down, than to worry about you and your problems. He won't hear you much less answer. Where do you think all this comes from? It's Satan because the Bible never says any of that! In fact, it's quite the opposite!

Satan can infiltrate your soul and create doubts that will send your prayers into a wall at 200 miles per hour. Why would he do that? It's because he knows what we sometimes forget! He understands that God the Father is on our side and our Father will help us. Then His help will cause others to see the difference your walk with Jesus has made in you, and subsequently create a spiritual curiosity in them that will draw them into a life with God.

Satan also knows that Christians, both individually and together in prayer, are powerful opposing forces that undue his evil plans. Our prayers can thwart his plans every time! Look at **Philippians 4:6-7,** *"Be anxious for nothing, but in everything by prayer and supplication with thanksgiving let your request be made known to God. And the peace of God which surpasses all comprehension shall guard your hearts and your mind in Christ Jesus."*

Why do our minds need to be guarded? Do you think you don't need to guard your heart and mind; that only things of value need to be guarded right? We are in a spiritual battle here. The front gates of every Army base have guards to protect the peace of the soldiers as they work and rest, but at any time they are training to go and fight the enemy. They are ready to be called into a deadly force to the enemy on a moment's notice. Are we? Are we training? Are we loyal? Are we ready to fight our spiritual enemy Satan at a moment's notice? Or are we half asleep with our guards down as he infiltrates our hearts and minds and then unloads on our most powerful weapon... Prayer?

Is prayer magic? No! God is not a genie that we summon from an ancient bottle. Prayer does not make demands when you ponder the difference between a request and a demand. It's easy to forget sometimes that God does not take orders from us. The Creator of all things doesn't need a thing from us! And if you want to go even deeper, whose benefit are our prayers for? We are the ones who need a relationship with God that is made possible with and by engaging with Jesus primarily through prayer.

Think about how you function when you are out of sync with Jesus and His calling on your life. The obvious answer is, "we don't function well at all." Where is that peace, that great sleep, that satisfied feeling as you watch the sun rise or set. We function best when we are in sync with God who is our Creator and our compass.

Are we going to suffer in this life? Yes! Prayer is not a barrier to suffering, so don't be surprised that suffering is coming. Or maybe for you, it's already here, or it happened already and your heart hurts beyond belief. Know that this is common to man, and you will get through it.

You really have two choices: Simply put, you can turn yourself inside out and be miserable; or you can rejoice in it knowing that every human before you has suffered in some way. But as Christians we know that everything has a purpose.

When I was barely in my 20s, I was involved with organized crime. I had the propensity to be an up-and-coming star in the world of crime. I met and was in awe of "made" men. Men who were ordained untouchable by an organization who would back anything they said or did to the point of murder. How did these men get so powerful? By proving themselves loyal, brave, dependable and trustworthy to the organizations they belonged. It would send chills down your spine when you were in their presence because you knew that they had the power to wipe anyone from the earth with a word.

We are the same, only stronger... much stronger if we serve the Most-High God. We are "made" men and women in a sense that we can change anything by aligning our actions and desires with that of God's. **1 Peter 4:12-13** tells us to not be surprised in suffering, but to rejoice in it. *"Brethren do not be surprised at the fiery ordeal among you, which comes upon you for a testing. As though some strange things were happening to you, but to the degree that you share the sufferings of Christ, keep on rejoicing so that also at the revelation of his glory, you may rejoice with exultation."*

Get it in your head that prayer is not a guarantee that you will not suffer! Suffering is a way to prove to us that we are not suffering for a worldly power like the "made" men I knew. Those "made" men all died miserable, young deaths at the hands of enemies or in prison. When we as Christians suffer, it is for Christ's sake.

Prayer is not an opportunity to show off. "Made" men never had to show off. You knew, and they knew it! The most important thing is that you need to have a rich prayer life. More simply put, a humble heart. **1 Peter 5:6** says, *"Humble yourselves, therefore under the mighty hand of God that he might exalt you at the proper time."*

Verse 7 goes on to say, *"Casting all your anxiety upon him, because he cares for you."*

So here we sit thinking, "What is it that separates the Christians from the non-Christians, and does it really matter?" The answer simply put is, "A personal one-on-one relationship with God's Son, Jesus Christ!" How does one get this relationship? By realizing that we are sinful creatures and confessing to Him that fact, and then asking Him for forgiveness. By asking Him to come into your life and change things, you are acknowledging the sacrifice He made for you on the cross. You are also opening the door to the Holy Spirit to come into your life and help you align your life to what He has had planned for you all along!

It basically says in **Romans 10:9**, *"With mouth man confesses and with heart man believes."* Too simple and abhorrent to non-Christians who would rather not humble themselves. But instead, continue to ram their heads into a wall daily and ignore the black hole in their hearts that is silently telling them they are missing the greatest things in life that nothing else can buy for them!

I have sat with many people at the time of their deaths all over the country, and almost all of them in their final reflections (who were non-Christians) were so scared of what was about to come that they begged for peace. A few tough guys and girls refused to humble themselves and sadly went into the next life unchanged and scared to death! But praise God there were those who asked for the answer to this puzzle, and they accepted Christ in their last breaths! Those were the ones who left with a smile, seeing the angels coming for them as they went!

And then there were those who I sat with that were indeed Christians, and even though they admitted they had made many mistakes, they left this world feeling so excited that they were about to see the Lord of lords face-to-face and they happily accepted their time here was done. For they knew with absolute confidence that the relationship which had started with a bended knee and humble heart was a profitable one and they had nothing to fear!

I prayed with all of them at the time and their last moments has made a difference in my life as I try and walk in this world worthy of the calling of a relationship to Jesus! It is not an easy task, but I can tell you as someone who was once a demon-possessed criminal who, at one time, lived by the creed that nothing matters and never slept a restful night, and that giving your heart and life over to Jesus and asking Him to forgive you and accepting His sacrifice on the cross, changed my life forever.

Maybe you're not quite ready yet. But just maybe some of you are ready to bend those knees and humble your hearts and ask for forgiveness, and I can help. It is so simple! First you need to admit that you have done wrong. Then ask Jesus to come into your heart and forgive you. Then confess **with your mouth and believe in your heart** that He died on the cross for you and rose again on the third day, and you will be saved from a life of darkness. The black hole of unsatisfaction will vaporize and no one can ever argue with you again that it is not real because you will have experienced it. And you will know God loves you and cares for you and wants to answer your prayers!

LET'S PRAY...

Today, Lord, open our hearts great Father for each other. Focus our attention on You and the mighty work You have for us. Let us look for great and mighty things from You. Each of us has needs, each of us must produce for our families, for our employees or employers, each of us must pay bills, each of us must perform for our family and friends, each of us are overwhelmed at times by it all. But we ask in the Mighty Name of Jesus that You strengthen us to be the kind of Spiritual Warriors You desire us to be and make a difference in the lives of others in our sphere of influence in our daily walk. Give us wisdom. Give us love. Give us Your eyes to see everyone around us like You see them, whether we like them or not. Keep us humble and moving in prayer and forgiveness with a purpose! In Jesus' Mighty Name. **AMEN**

CHAPTER THREE

Prayer and Forgiveness

Secular psychologists generally define forgiveness as a conscious, deliberate decision to release feelings of resentment or vengeance toward a person or group who has harmed you, regardless of if they actually deserve your forgiveness. So why is it important to forgive and how does this affect your prayers?

Before I became a Christian, I was full of hatred and anger, and I would never forgive anyone who hurt me or crossed me. I was known for vengeance and would do anything to square up people who did me wrong. My father left our family when I was 13 and, as the oldest, I had to take his role. I hated him for it and wouldn't talk to him for years. I sold drugs and put a lot of weed and cocaine on the streets on credit, and I rarely got screwed because the streets knew I specialized in revenge!

As a young man learning the car business, I quickly started to understand that everyone was out for themselves and would stab you in the back the second you turned around. One of the ways you protected yourself was to either stab them first or to retaliate on them with extreme violence. I preferred the extreme violence! I believe that letting go of revenge was one of the hardest things I had on my "to do" list from God.

I learned that "revenge is a dish best served cold", and I was a master chef at that dish! Why did that matter, when the truth is, it didn't? Back then I was a devout atheist and never prayed about anything. Well, except one time when I got robbed buying $5000 of weed by a feigning, heroin addict in Logan Heights, San Diego's Compton. This guy stuffed a sawed off, double barrel 12 gauge in my mouth and pulled the trigger. At that instant, with my eyes wide open and looking into the hate in his eyes, I silently said two words, "Jesus, no!" I know why I couldn't talk. He had busted my bottom teeth and the gun was in my mouth. I was backed up to a wall of a house between bushes where the ambush was set up. It misfired and I spit some broken teeth out of my mouth. Then I made a beeline toward the street because I was unarmed... Stupid!

I heard the hammer drop again and the blast from that beast of a gun, and I literally dove for the street. Amazingly all the shots went around me and rejoined itself as it bounced down the street in the dark, sparking like sparklers every time they hit the pavement. Not one pellet hit me, not even the bottom of my shoes! I got up and ran to my car which was parked down the street.

Then I went and got some guys and guns, and we went back and found the heroin addict that shot at me, and I got my revenge. That night was a very bad night!

I think it's fair to say that as Christians we are expected to forgive. Think about it. You can't become a Christian without instantly getting involved with the whole concept. Why do I say that? Because to become a Christian means to have a personal relationship with Jesus. In order to do this, you have to confess your sins. Then you ask Him to forgive you and believe that as the Son of God, He can do that. You also believe that He was raised from the dead (see **Romans 10:9**).

We start our Christian life by asking for forgiveness of sins. But we are born sinners, and we will constantly sin every day, either in thought, word, or deed. We are always asking God to forgive us. It's even in the Lord's Prayer when Jesus teaches His disciples how to pray (**Luke 11:1-4**). Forgiveness is a basic tenant of the Christian life and a great way to display the love of Christ to the world. The reason we hate to do it is because, from the world's standpoint, it is weakness! Yet it is one of the quickest ways to show God you're improving and listening and maturing and learning how to give those tough people and situations over to Him, instead of taking matters into your own hands. By not forgiving, it will also hinder your prayers being heard.

Unforgiveness is a quick way to poison yourself to death! I once heard that hating on someone is like drinking poison and expecting someone else to die. It affects your heart and soul and it's a major gun in Satan's armory. If the devil can keep you angry and hating, then you will not be worth a darn as a Christ follower! But let's get back to prayer...

Here is my basic question. How do you expect God to forgive you for anything if you go on not forgiving those who have hurt you? **Mark 11:25** says specifically, *"And whenever you stand praying, forgive, if you have anything against anyone, so that your father also who is in heaven may forgive your transgressions."* **Mathew 6: 14-15** also says, *"For if you forgive men, for their transgressions your heavenly father will also forgive you but if you do not forgive then your father will not forgive your transgressions."* How do you expect God to listen to you seriously and answer your prayers if you are an angry, unforgiving person?

It even goes so much deeper when you read **Mathew 18:21-22.** Peter, God's star disciple, was asking Jesus how many times should we forgive a person? Typical human thinking... looking for ways to satisfy God and still be able to hold onto our unforgiveness. Kind of funny when you think about it, and it was typical Peter. But Jesus' answer was epic. The custom of the day was to forgive three times. In **Matthew 18:21-22,** Then Peter came to him saying, *"Lord how often shall my brother sin against me, and I forgive him? Up to seven times?" Jesus answered, "I do not say up to seven times but up to seventy times seven."* That's 490 times! In other words, who do you know that has sinned against you almost 500 times in your life and is still around? I doubt anyone. What Jesus was saying is, "There is no real number of times that forgiveness doesn't matter. God doesn't expect you to forgive. He actually demands that you forgive, especially if you want your prayers heard.

When you really think about this, we sin countless times in our life, both as Christians and before we became Christians, and all it takes for God to forgive us is for us to ask. I know I am a million times past 7x70 in my sin count, and God still looks at me as forgiven when I sincerely confess my sins and turn away from my sin-life patterns. If you only sinned three times a day and live to be 75, that is 82,125 sins committed, and I don't think there is a person walking the earth who doesn't sin at least that, whether in thought, word, or deed. Heck, back in my old days, I probably sinned that many times in one day!

Go back to **Matthew 6:14-15**, and remember, *"If you forgive, He forgives! If you don't, He doesn't!"* Not a hard concept to understand, but a hard one to live! Especially without the Holy Spirit living inside your heart. By having a heart of unforgiveness you are thinking more highly of yourself than you should. You have been given grace. Grace is receiving forgiveness when you don't deserve it. **Romans 12:3** (paraphrased), Paul says, *"Don't think more highly of yourself because you have been given grace!"* Simply put, if you want your prayers to be answered, you must learn how to forgive!

When my ex-wife left me eight years ago, it broke my heart and caused an enormous amount of anger. In fact, it was enough anger to bring my old ways back. I had been planning to use extreme violence again against the man she ran off with. In a phone call, I begged him not to take her away. He "spit in my face" telling me to pound sand, and said, "She's hot and if she wants to be with me that is her choice, not mine."

After 33 years as a Christian, and 25 years of being a faithful husband and father, a Bible teacher, a Light in an evil business; after sharing the gift of grace with countless lost car salesmen, I was getting ready to commit the ultimate crime. I planned it perfectly, and I knew I was capable and experienced enough to inflict deadly force in that mode. But God reached out to me through my loving Apache brother Homer, and Homer told me whatever I was planning, that God told him to call me and invite me to the reservation to heal.

Homer urged me not to take my revenge, but to trust God and sell what I had left and come work the cattle ranch. Funny that the ranch is called Slaughter Cattle Ranch. Homer did not know what I was planning. He was only offering an escape from the pain. I had told no one because when you are about to do something that heinous, the only one you can trust is yourself!

Go ask all the mafia guys in prison if this isn't true. People will always do what's best for them when the crap hits the fan, and they have a choice... you or them. Anyway, I prayed and asked God to forgive me, and I did what Homer said. I sold everything and left Reno. I took my dog, my son, who had just gotten out of prison, and all my hunting equipment.

Sadly, on the way to the ranch, my dog was killed. I loved that dog and I remember that day well as I buried her by the Kern River where I had trained her. I was bawling as I looked upward to Heaven, and I cried out, "God why? My wife I love, my possessions, my family, my career, and now even my beloved dog. All gone. Why?" I cried and cried.

Shortly after, a song called, "Let Her Go" came on the radio by a band named Passenger. The lyrics say, "You only know you love her when you let her go. And you let her go." That song still makes me cry every time I hear it. Yet I knew that God was using all of this change in my life to bring me back to Him!

To let go of my wife is to forgive. To forgive means to heal. To forgive is a character builder that God has in His plans. Revenge may be best served cold, but forgiveness is served steaming hot and dripping with the savory gravy of God's love!

As a result of all that pain and suffering, God led me to a new place in my life where I could continue to lead unsaved men in my new home. He gave me a new vision of what it meant to forgive on a level that I had never understood. He led me to other Christian men who helped me to get back on my feet and to help start a wonderful new church in Reno.

Even to this day, He is blessing me in a new town with new purpose and new friends. We never see this coming in the storm, but if we practice the very opposite of what the world tells us to do, we will be blessed and the people around us who witnessed our faith will be blessed to by our example. Over time, your surrender to forgiveness will certainly align your will to His and you will see God move on your prayers!

LET'S PRAY...

Father in Heaven, forgive me for my sin. Give me Your grace and grant me unmerited favor because I do not deserve it. I believe Your Son came to this earth for the one purpose. And that was to live a perfect life in human flesh, be tempted in all the ways we are tempted, and yet without sin. As we give our lives to Him in thankfulness, Father. Protect my heart from making the same mistake over and over. Give me the sound judgement to forgive those who have hurt me and forgive those who plan evil against me. You control all things in my life, and You are always faithful to give me the strength to trust You in all things, even to learn how to forgive endlessly because that is the meaning of 7x70! Forgive me, Lord, as I have forgiven those who have hurt me! Hear my prayers, Father, because I ask these things according to Your will, not mine. And I ask them in the Mighty Name of Jesus Christ, Your Son and My Savior! **AMEN**

CHAPTER FOUR

Prayer and Adversity

How many times have you talked to someone, and they tell you, "Man, I'm going through some real tough times?" What are tough times? Those depressing valleys we fall into, the failures we are experiencing in jobs, relationships or financially. The dictionary defines adversity as a state or instance of serious or continued difficulty or misfortune.

All of us face many types of adversity, and as humans there are commonalities in the way we handle it. Again, you can try and justify that bad luck has caught up with you, or you can look for a deeper purpose in it that will give you hope to endure the season and come out of it stronger.

I have counseled a lot of people because I have made my Christian stand public at work. I have been selling cars for 50 years and have been a Christian for 40 of that. I let people know I am a Christian and that I believe exactly what a Born-again Christian is supposed to believe. I try with great effort not to behave like I'm not a Christian because the people who do not believe are always looking to point out the hypocrisy of Christians who don't act like Christians. That is never more prevalent than when hard times hit us—when we are crushed and fighting some battle.

I have been ridiculed a million times on car lots for being Christian, and I accept the ribbing and descent. In fact, I enjoy it because the Bible says that, "If you suffer for His sake, you are doing something right." However, the cool part of letting these people know is that when tough times come, the same ones who love to make fun of you will come to you alone, to seek your advice and help when adversity hits them. They long for faith and help in tough times and there is a Grand Canyon of difference.

Adversity can beat you down and cause you to feel sorry for yourself. You get angry and doubt if anything is even worth the effort. It will make you seek temporary escapes like alcohol, drugs, sex addictions, gambling. You can try to ignore it, and take off to go fishing, or get online and spend some money shopping, but none of that is going to fix it. And withdrawing and cursing God isn't going to fix it either. Too many Christians are like this.

When they became a Christian, maybe they were suffering from some of these things and the Holy Spirit moved on them. They accepted Christ and gained freedom. They moved into a new position as a believer and began to learn the ways of the Bible and started going to church and making Christian friends. Then some really good feelings and temporary success of what they have been struggling with starts to fall apart, and they fall down the same hole, and they lose their faith in God. It is easy for them to take a U-turn away from God because it's familiar territory. We love to be where we've been. It's a dark side of our personalities.

The funny thing is that adversity turns us to prayer, too. We can be quick to look up and say, "God, I don't need this right now. Please fix this, quick!" We are programmed to fix. But God has a purpose in everything, and for us to survive hard times we must attempt to understand what God is trying to do with us in this obviously ordained adversity. Our lives are a constantly changing roller coaster of peaks and valleys.

I have made so much money in my life at times and it seemed I could do no wrong and that it would never end. Between the time I quit being a professional criminal at age 27, up until the age of 35, I had saved and invested about 3 million dollars selling Toyotas and racing cars. I could do nothing wrong; I had the Midas touch. I was so successful I started to believe my own BS. I became so prideful that I started making mistakes that would ultimately bring down my fortune streak.

I was making character mistakes; I was having a real hard time in my first marriage, and so I started being unfaithful thinking I was justified. Oh, yea and I was a Christian, as well as a successful businessman! I spoke at Christian businessmen lunches and taught a large Sunday school of 200 adults every week at church. I witnessed to guys struggling all the time. I had "Racers for Christ" patches on my driving suit and on my race car. I was famous in

LA, and behind it all, I was fighting a sexual addiction and having sex with every hot girl I came across.

I had unlimited money and power. I felt like I was invincible and invisible when I would cross the line. Unlike Job in the Bible, who didn't seem to deserve the beatings that God let Satan give him, I did deserve the beatings that I got! I made choices that eventually traded all that money, fame, and power in for pride and lust. God allowed me to be sifted by turning my financial life around and I suffered a catastrophic loss at age 37.

Everything was gone! All the money I had saved... gone! All the property and possessions... gone! Divorce number 1, and it was a nasty one. I was being sued. People were stealing what little I had to live on. People I owed wanted to kill me. All my fair-weather friends were gone and sadly most of my Christian friends walked on me. I was even facing financial criminal charges of being out of trust, and possible jail time.

One day I was sitting in my bedroom in my condo hiding out at night and fell into the darkest depression. I had smoked some weed and was drinking; I hadn't smoked weed in seven years because I was dedicated to being as mentally and physically in shape as possible in my racing career. But that night I broke it all, and by myself. I think I was even drinking tequila from a bottle of some expensive boutique liquor that someone had given me. Tequila never ends good for me... ever!

Sitting there in the dark on the edge of my bed, I had about as much adversity as anyone can face. That was when I decided to see if God wanted me dead, too. I had my model 29 Smith and Wesson 44 mag loaded and sitting on the bed next to me. I unloaded it in the dark—240 grain magnum hollow points. I spun the cylinder and flipped it shut knowing it was unloaded. A true game of Russian roulette. I put it to my temple and pulled the trigger. I wanted to see what it felt like on a dry run. I flinched even though I knew it was unloaded. So, I practiced pulling back the hammer on that fierce cannon and squeezing that trigger over and over until it was smooth. Every time I pulled it, I remember thinking it was a cowardly way out to my kids and my mother! But I was so beat and so defeated and so twisted that I truly believed I couldn't face the world a loser, broke and shamed.

So here I go... I was always fascinated with Russian roulette and had watched guys play this game for huge money like the movie, "The Deer Hunter", years before with my criminal uncle in Tijuana, MX. I loaded one 240 grain hollow point in the cylinder. Then I spun it and slammed it shut and put it to my head just as I had practiced.

The bedroom was completely dark, and I did not see where the bullet ended its rotation. I could hear the finely tuned gears spinning and the unmistakable sound of the cylinder locking into place in its perfectly, machined cradle in that huge pistol frame. I reached for the hammer with my thumb and pulled it back, click, click, click, ever so slowly. My finger, my right index finger, was on the trigger, and it had a very light pull. You see, just weeks before, I had that gun to a gunsmith who completely reworked everything. Why? Because I could. I had money and was bored. Bored with life's challenges and I could spend money on stupid things like customizing a perfect gun so I could show it off to my friends who also had too many guns and too much money.

Anyway, this beautiful 44 mag was loaded with one bullet that was the most powerful handgun in the world at that time. Its barrel was pressed into my temple with a fair amount of pressure like I had practiced, and my strongest finger was resting on the final piece of the puzzle… the final choice to play the final gamble. I sat a while, and the tequila and drugs took over.

My adversities were too much to handle. I had cursed myself by all my bad behavior and now God was done with me. I thought of my son Tommy who had been the catalyst of bringing me to Christ just eight years earlier. I thought of my baby girl Kacie who I loved, and my brothers, my mother, and even my dog. But I decided in the end they would all be better off without me.

I squeezed it perfectly and, in a millisecond, it clicked! The horror of what I had just done hit me like a sudden car wreck. I flinched and instantly threw the gun at the wall; I remember getting about a half a thought of "What were you thinking?" when the gun hit the corner of the wall in the bedroom and fired! The flames came out the barrel three feet and in a millisecond the bullet grazed my hair and passed by my head and through the roof of the condo. I had played Russian roulette twice in one try, and I leapt up and ran out the front door. I bolted to my car and sped off in utter amazement. I wasn't dead!

I was shaking all over and completely sober. I drove a few minutes to an industrial area and parked and wept uncontrollably. It was there that I realized God wasn't done with me. I begged

His forgiveness. And for a long time after, I sat and prayed. My confession was thorough, and I asked Him for another chance to approach life with courage to face the utter financial destruction I was in.

I don't care if you're just having a hard time, or if you're facing complete disaster. Before you go off the deep end and listen to the enemy that all is lost, learn to pray! Start the prayers the minute you begin to feel defeated, not later. Especially after taking drugs and alcohol! God is always interested in seeing your reaction to hard times. That's why He tests us. He doesn't let bad things happen to us with the goal of failing us. It's actually the opposite. He allows tough times and real adversity to bring us through and cement our hearts to Him and His solutions for our lives.

I am always sad when I hear of someone intentionally killing themselves, but I understand how it can happen. I wish I could have talked to them before it was too late and share the satisfaction when you trust God and get through it. In **James 1**, the entire chapter has been a "go to" chapter for me ever since that fateful night. It explains the purpose God has for us when we suffer adversity, and He tells us if we lack wisdom to ask, but to ask with a believing heart!

In **James 1:2-6,** *"Consider it all joy my brethren when you encounter various trials, knowing that the testing of your faith produces endurance, and let endurance have its perfect result, that you may be perfect and complete, lacking in nothing. But if any of you lacks wisdom, let him ask of God* **(in other words, pray)** *who gives to all men generously and without reproach and it will be given to him. But let him ask in faith* *without doubting for the one who doubts is like the surf of the sea, driven and tossed by the wind."*

As a result of that disaster, I remarried a beautiful woman, got back on my feet running other men's businesses. I had three more beautiful children who, to this day some 28 years later, have become my best friends and biggest blessings along with my first two children. And I also have three incredible grandchildren.

God has used all my failures in life to help others and looking back I am so grateful that night passed as a memory instead of an epitaph!

LET'S PRAY...

Lord God, Master of all things. We ask You in total faith, without a sliver of doubt, to give us wisdom and to let us in on the big picture of life. Give us the strength to trust our lessons that You allow us to make. Those lessons that help draw us closer to You. And give us a fire that will allow us to make it through as stronger, more mature Christians... braver and fearless as the challenges in the world come at us. Give us eyes and hearts to be bold to the lost and hurting people around us who suffer from the same things we have been through. Give us hearts to care for ourselves. In Jesus' Mighty Name and Power, we ask for a natural reaction of turning to prayer and trusting in You in adversity. **AMEN**

CHAPTER FIVE

Prayer and Temptation

Are any of you struggling with an area of sin? Kind of a silly question when you consider we are human, and the only person to ever have lived a sinless life was Jesus. He was sent here for that purpose... to be born of flesh from a woman and carry out a sinless life, so that He may become the ultimate, one-time final sacrifice to provide us all with a way to reunite with God and His kingdom. So yes, we all suffer with some kind of sin, and it's a sin to not admit it!

1 John 1:9-10 says, *"If you confess your sins, he is just to forgive you and if you say you have no sin you are a liar, and the truth is not in you."* What are some of the obvious sins we struggle with in this life? Well, you have common sins like improper sexual thoughts or actions, drugs, and alcohol, greed, money, power, idols, such as shopping. Then you have the not so obvious ones like anger and hatred, resentment, covetousness, and those things you can smile away to other people while your heart stews hatred at them.

Why is this such a problem with all of us? Why can't God just make it easier and fix this, so we don't have to? Adam and Eve blew us all into the weeds of struggle until God sent His Son to open a pathway back to Him. But if you really look at the big picture, we are (whether we like it or not) soldiers in a spiritual war. We either realize it and get in the battles in front of us, or we choose to become helpless victims being slaughtered like innocent children when the bullets fly.

Galatians 5:17-21 says, *"For the flesh sets its desires against the Spirit and the Spirit against the flesh for these are in opposition to each other, so that you may not do the things that you please but if you are led by the Spirit, you are not under the Law. Now the deeds of the flesh are evident, which are immorality, impurity, sensuality, idolatry, sorcery, enmities, strife, jealousy, outbursts, of anger, disputes, dissensions fractions, envy, drunkenness, carousing, and things like these of which I forewarn you just as I have forewarned you that those who practice such things shall not inherit the kingdom of God."*

Man, that's quite a list! And it's a hard one not to find a least a couple of things we are not guilty of… if not all. But notice at the end of that list it says, *"those who practice"*. If you want to get good at one of those, it takes practice! Are you practicing at, let's say drunkenness? Maybe you practice outbursts of anger, and are known for having a short fuse? Maybe you read tarot cards and go see a fortune teller once in a while to get your spiritual compass on course? Or maybe you practice silent, sex acts with every hot girl you see or every hot guy that smiles at you?

You see, this is not a mystery and it is obvious that the Spirit and the flesh are at war! The Spirit and your desires are enemies. It's easy to be losing this war at all times because we think (and it's part of the lie) that God tempts us. He tortures us to show us that we are weak. Is this true? Look at **James 1:13-15**, *"Let no one say when he is tempted, I am being tempted by God, for God cannot be tempted by evil, nor does He himself tempt anyone. But each one is tempted when he is carried away by his own lust. Then when lust is conceived, it gives birth to sin; and when sin is accomplished, it brings forth death."* Death, in this instance, means separation from God.

Are we unique in this problem? Are we to float out here trying to see how weak we are as individuals not knowing that every human, every man, and woman suffer with this? **1 Corinthians 10:13** tells us that, *"No temptation has overtaken you that is not common to man; but God is faithful who will not allow you to be tempted more than you are able, but with the temptation will also provide you an escape so that you may be able to endure."*

It is common to struggle with temptations, but it is also possible to overcome them. You get good at them by practicing them, and you can beat them by practicing beating them. Baby steps of which the first step is realizing I have a problem; the second step is realizing I need to stop trying to be good at being bad. Stop practicing them! The third baby step is starting to look for the escape hatch that God promises to give you and is always there.

The last step is getting your guns loaded for the battle you are in with real spiritual bullets... Prayer!

I had a problem running to sexual sin all the time when I was a younger and stronger man. I knew I shouldn't call that girl and I would call anyway. Low and behold her line was busy or she didn't answer, so there was my escape hatch. I had a choice to move on and go do something else, instead of running toward sexual sin. But what did I do time after time? I kept calling back until I got an answer, or I'd call her friends and find out where she was, or maybe even call the next one on my list, until I got what my flesh wanted... a sexual fix! I blew past my escape hatches and sadly ran to sin.

When I hear men of God being shamed from affairs with their secretaries, I wonder how many escape hatches they blew past. It's a big thing for the enemy to take down a pastor in sexual sin. The world loves it and takes every opportunity to attack the church.

I had a pastor friend who started a ministry helping fallen pastors with their lust and secret sins. He was overwhelmed with requests from every corner of the globe with every kind of sexual deviation from professional priests, pastors, and reverends who were desperately seeking help. They blew by the escape hatches God had provided for them and fell victim to the guns of the enemy. It was sad to hear and eventually that pastor himself wound up divorced and off track.

So how do we defend ourselves? My mafia uncle used to tell me, "Give yourself a chance to win." It was epic-life advice that I always got from him. If you are constantly struggling, then look around you. Who are you hanging out with? Who takes you down? **1 Corinthians 15:33** says, *"Do not be misled. Bad company corrupts good character."* Being tempted is never going to go away. But choosing to use your Spiritual power to ask for God's help before you sin, instead of going invisible and then using prayer to ask God for forgiveness! Wow what a concept.

Mathew 26:41, Jesus tells his crew, *"Watch and pray so that you will not fall into temptation. The spirit is willing, but the flesh is weak."* Do you get that Jesus our Savior understands how hard it is for us, because He lived in our world both as a man tempted in all the things? We are tempted, yet He used prayer and talked to His Father to overcome and not sin. Can't we at least try and do the same? Can't we go to prayer quicker; can't we jump through the escape hatch at least once in a while before we keep forcing ourselves into evil? Can't we pray that we give ourselves a chance to win? Even professional criminals understand this concept!

The same verses in **Mark 14:35** say to, *"Keep awake, keep watching, pray"* and **Luke 22:40**, *"Pray that you may not enter into temptation."* I think that most of us think temptation is like something that happens to us that we cannot control. But all of the eyewitness accounts written by three disciples say Jesus said to pray so you don't enter, like we have to enter temptation to sin. To be tempted is **not** a sin, but to enter **is** a sin! Give yourself a chance to win by praying first!

LET'S PRAY...

Lord, give me help from my temptations. You know what I am facing today. My spirit is weak, and I need the Holy Spirit to fill me with Your strength and power. Your word says my weakness is Your strength. The Bible says I will not be tempted beyond my strength. Please, Lord, don't let me be dragged down like a wild animal caught in a trap to evil by my sinful desires. Your power is greater than the power of Satan who controls evil in this world and in my mind. Show me the escape hatches. Show me the safe way out. And give me the wherewithal to use it and live to fight another day for You. Give me the wisdom to learn Your word, to read my Bible daily, and to understand that the fear of the Lord is the beginning of understanding wisdom. Thank You, Lord, for everyone who is reading this and praying this prayer now. Use them. Bless them. Keep them clean from sin. Use them mightily in their homes and in their jobs and with their friends. In Christ Holy Name, I pray. **AMEN**

CHAPTER SIX

Prayer and Self-Control

The definition of self-control: "the ability to control oneself, in particular one's emotions and desires or the expression of them in one's behavior, especially in difficult situations." As a Christian, I believe that self-control is being able to say, "No" to the thoughts and behaviors that are counter to being a good person, a person whose word is good. It's a person who displays integrity when no one is looking. Because they understand that Someone is always looking. Someone or something is always watching.

Spiritual beings are always watching us. Angels are watching the boundaries that God has set on the demons who are watching us and devising ways to get us to lose our self-control. The sinful nature we are born with needs to be corralled, but first we must muster the courage through prayer to gain a foothold to climb or free ourselves.

Recently I became emotionally involved with a much younger woman. Everyone who loved me advised against it. We had many decades between us but despite that, we connected on a deeper level. Cody Jinx sings a song "Must Be the Whiskey." The words describe exactly how I felt at the beginning of this relationship. "Lately I'm going crazy, my heart says to love you, but my head tells me to run. My head and my heart seem to be a million miles apart. Must be the whiskey." Well, I don't drink so I can't blame it on the whiskey! So why did I lose my self-control and fall in love with her? I knew from the beginning it had almost no chance to work. I knew my daughters would protest. Heck, my oldest girl was older than her!

What drove me to this girl was a spiritual connection that was rooted in the unusual spiritual maturity she had. Also, in me, there was a deep loneliness for a relationship that was real and still is to this day! As we started down this road, we had to sneak in our times together. She had a roommate, and we weren't going there. And I had two of my kids living with me, so we weren't going there. We parked around town in my truck and talked for hours.

I finally came clean to my kids and brought her in my family. I was so proud of them for embracing her with a Christian spirit that I had trained them with in their lives. But she never reciprocated. I never met her parents or her brother. He was going to meet me once but then changed his mind. I think she was getting pushed back from all of them and couldn't gain the courage to take us to the next step with her family. That hurt in a way that I knew from the start could happen. She also didn't want to go public with our relationship with the common friends and group we shared.

I sought advice from my pastor, and he said crazier things happen in love and encouraged me to follow my heart, but to maintain boundaries by not having sex with her outside of marriage. To her credit she was very disciplined in this area and knew I had leadership responsibilities in the church that I was not going to violate by example. She did her part mostly to contain the desire we had for a physical relationship. She was not comfortable with going public with it and wanted to continue in secret. Let me say I would have married her in a second because I truly loved her personality, her spiritual awareness, and our time together was always a joy!

One day I took her to some ancient petroglyphs not far from Reno that no one could find or go to without the level of access I have, or the outdoor experience I possess from hunting and guiding hunters in Northern Nevada. She was blown away by the over 2000 rock drawings in this one canyon. It was a special day for both of us.

While hiking around the rock art, I stepped on a rock and, as I did, the rock rolled onto my other foot and pinned me to the ground. This bolder was massive, and I was truly stuck in a terrible situation. She wasn't far and I called out to her to come see what I had done. As she looked at my foot being crushed by the bolder and realizing how far in we were, with no help in sight, and no way for her to get help because she would never find her way out in my Kawasaki Mule.

We were out of cell range by miles and miles, and I could tell she felt a huge moment of anxiety. I had trapped myself in an impossible situation in one careless step. I prayed knowing that I needed a miracle to free myself. As I bent over this rock which I could barely get my arms around and lifted with key power, a power I had mastered learning to become a black belt in Hwa Rang Do many years before, she watched as I did the impossible. I lifted this rock just enough to pull my boot out! It was a superhuman display of strength and she was blown away.

As I look back on our year together, I think God was showing me that I had no business being with her. She wanted kids. I had raised five. She was ashamed to come out with our relationship. I was not! I was pinned in a situation that had no good ending! God gave me the strength to finally end it.

I had purposefully stayed away from her in my guiding season as I had about six weeks in the mountains with hunters, one after another. One day she started to try and break it off because I know she felt trapped. I made up some excuse, but she felt it and was going to use that as a pivot point to separate. I didn't argue. I told her I loved her but couldn't continue without getting married and going public. She cried and I acted tough (but only on the outside). I told her I had been through many tougher things than ending our relationship. When I left her apartment that night, I cried, and to this day I miss her. She made up an excuse that she called our misfortune a case of "life timing." We matched as a couple in every area of life except our age.

Everyone on my side was right from the start. I went all in

anyway and, in the end, we were both hurt! Self-Control! Must be the whiskey of desire! Yes, Cody Jinx. Go listen to that song and you will laugh or cry as I have done a million times. Now we are distant friends, and I pray for her to find a young man who can give her the baby she deserves and a life to raise that kid which I could have never done. She was so special, and I should have had more self-control from the start. I pinned myself to the ground. My heart was stuck under a boulder that only a miracle could move. And He did.

There are many other things we all struggle with in the area of self-control like food, drinking, greed, shopping, money, lust, sex, hobbies and all of them can consume us if we are weak in this area. We all know when we are going too deep, but we go in anyway. Why? It's seductive and common to man. As we become enveloped in lack of self-control, we start to suffer the consequences that comes with a lack of self-control. We become slaves to them. And with time they become overwhelming and consume our potential to do God's work for us. They create a level of guilt as well that will paralyze us from being productive.

Proverbs 25:28 says, *"Like a city that is broken into without walls is the man who has no control over his spirit."* Learning how to have self-control is and being in a state of self-control is the very foundation of living a righteous and selfless life that reflects the Spirit of Jesus and an awareness for what He has done for you.

When I was young, my dad used to tell me and my brothers, "Do what I say, not what I do," as he was cussing, or drinking or kissing the neighbor's wife, but it always made me angry and made me not want to listen to him. We don't have that excuse with our Heavenly Father because He expresses that our actions are more important than our words. He tells us what really matters is the condition of our heart. If our hearts are given to Him, then we will want to control our human passions and display a level of behavior to the world around us that brings Him and all Christians honor.

If you need help in this area, then take it seriously and start memorizing scripture about self-control. The Bible says much on this, and there are many Bible characters who struggled with it to study, some failures like David and some champions like Paul.

Again, we go back to the most powerful underrated weapon we have... Prayer. Take baby steps in the right direction and pray for God to give you the ability to find the escape hatch He always provides, and to keep finding them time after time until you start to look for them before you even get close to falling.

I have counseled many car salesmen who were struggling with addictions, and I always volunteered to be available for them 24/7 to call if they we going to fall. They wouldn't and they would fall, and then they would be back crying, "Why can't I get my act together?" After a while I would just tell them, "Don't come back to me until you are serious about fixing your lack of self-control. I don't have time to babysit you and try and make you feel better after you screw up."

That seems harsh and it speaks to my human lack of compassion with weak, repeat offenders. But there is an element of truth to it. You have to want to fix it first. You have to want to be a person of honor. You make the first move and fortunately God will always answer your prayer. Do you think He is going to say, "No, I don't want you to have self-control?" I doubt it!

LET'S PRAY...

My Lord of all strength and mercy, what an area of growth You have set before us and what a wonderful reality it is that You set Your angels around us from falling too far from You. You expect us to do our part in controlling our desires and not turning them into evil actions. A true challenge we are capable of **if** we use the power of the Holy Spirit and fling our hearts into action as soon as we start off the deep end. Give us the strength, Lord, to take this incredible human challenge seriously and to gain wisdom and foresight into the bad life results that will come when we lose self-control. It never ends good. Give us a desire to equip ourselves with weapons of the Spirit and the courage to fight the most important battles we face... the ones within us. In Your Son's Precious and Holy Name. **AMEN**

CHAPTER SEVEN

Prayer and Self-Respect

To have self-respect means to hold yourself in proper esteem. It means believing you are good and worthy of being treated well by others and, surprisingly, by yourself! There are so many factors that help us develop good self-respect as we grow as people. The way our parents treated us as kids has a huge effect on how we look at ourselves as teens where, in my opinion, we start to gain independence and, depending on the framework in us, we start to make bad decisions. Young people need to gain acceptance in a desperate way and will stumble down any path to find it, any form of self-respect.

If our parents had poor self-images, it is easily transferred to us. Young girls will give up their virginity to find love from a boy that makes them feel accepted and loved. Young boys will start a life of crime and compromise to hook up with a bunch of boys that accept them into another tribe. We are tribal by nature and find comfort in others liking us. And we will do anything to gain it especially when our self-image is twisted. This is all rooted in our sin nature and without really good parents constantly giving us a feeling of self-worth, it is easy to get on life's path with a crippled sense of self-respect.

Our sin nature and the damage from the way we allow others to treat us all contribute to our lack of self-respect, and the consequences can be devastating. Depression, constant questioning, anger, feelings of unworthiness, distance from family and friends and compromising in unproper relationships all contribute to a downward spiral in how we view ourselves. I believe a lot of addictions have their roots dug deep into our souls as a result of trying to escape the pain of a poor self-image.

Back when I had limitless money and power and did not believe in God, I could spot women with low self-respect in a flash. I would complement them and watch their eyes to judge just how desperate they were for attention. My goal was to have sex with them. In those days, it really didn't matter to me what I was about to do to them would further reduce their self-respect because I was a selfish sex addict who needed his fix, and they were hot.

I could see the desperation in married women whose husbands ignored them or put them down. I could see girls who had terrible fathers who left them or mistreated their mothers. I was a master at putting them together. The results of a lack of self-respect are endless. When you lack self-respect your self-image bar is low, and you will sin easily. You fall into deep depression and constant questioning of your life and the people around you who just keep biting off parts of you and leaving you to bleed to death. You become angry and the feelings of unworthiness force you into situations where you trade your integrity for money or acceptance. You make the wrong friends who are also miserable in this area because misery loves company. You distance yourself from family and friends who don't seem to understand and have nothing to offer except advice like "you need to get your life together." Relationships suffer and breakdown and you flee into the dark night of compromise.

When I was involved in crime, my uncle controlled most of the prostitution in San Diego. He had men who ran this business, and they were heartless dogs. He had one guy named Broadway Joe whose job was to sit at the bus station on Broadway Street in San Diego and watch for young run-away girls. Young teens were big money to the sex addicts who would pay exorbitant amounts of money to have sex with teenagers! He would watch and see a young runaway get off the bus and usually they would have just one bag. They would start to walk down the street alone because no one was there to pick them up. The looks on their faces would tell him they were scared and alone a million miles from their homes and parents. Whatever led them to run was about to turn into the biggest horror story of their young lives.

Broadway Joe, who looked like Captain Kangaroo in a

vested suit, would drive up on them in his Cadillac and start a conversation and offer to help them. He never missed as this was his con and, once he had them, the terror began. He would take them and, in a matter of a week, turn them into heroin addicts, and shortly after, street girls of the night. But before they got to the street, all the perverted mafia guys got their shot first.

I was too busy learning how to be a 24/7 criminal and sex was just something we all did to relieve the stress. I felt so bad in my soul when I would hear Broadway Joe bragging about these girls. I'd wait my turn with the new ones, and then I would snatch them and tell them I would get them out. Then I would buy them a ticket and help them to escape!

I sent many of them packing home, and after a while it became apparent to the other men who was doing this. I was caught right after I put a beautiful, little 15-year-old Italian girl back on a plane to Cleveland.

The beating I took with a baseball bat was merciless, but I took it, and I was much more careful in the future when helping these young runaways to escape a certain young death to heroin, sex abuse and slavery. I listened to their stories of how unloving their parents were to them. I looked into the pain in their eyes and saw total lack of self-respect, as they were now being forced into have fat old men lay on them.

I was on the car lot one summer day and a real mafia looking "Tony Soprano" character in a suit came up on me and surprised me. He said, "Are you Tommy?" I jumped because that didn't happen to me often. I was on home turf and safe, but he looked like a hit man, and for a second, I thought, "Oh, no, I just got made and this is it." I said, "Yea, why?" He reached into his coat, and I started to move toward him quickly, looking around for who might help me not to get shot. Then he pulled out an envelope and handed it to me, and I stopped dead in my tracks.

"This is for you," he said, and he told me his name. "I flew here from Cleveland to come thank you for sending my daughter home and helping her escape. I, too, am a part of things like this, but she is everything in the world to me, and I will never let her get that far off the deep end again. When she ran away, I prayed, and I don't normally pray. But God answered my prayer with you, so I came here for one purpose. To thank you, and to give you this gift for saving my daughter." I was speechless. He turned and walked away. Then he got into a waiting cab and disappeared forever.

I didn't dare to look in the envelope then, so I stashed it and looked later. There was $5000 cash inside. That was a lot of money in 1971! So, I guess you can say that the baseball bat beating had a good ending. I was hurting a lot of people in those days and in many bad ways, but somehow helping those young teenage girls escape a life of drug addiction and prostitution made me have some degree of self-respect.

In **Mathew 22:37**, Jesus is talking about the most important commandments to the religious leaders of the day, and they ask Him which commandment is greatest. Jesus says, *"Love the Lord your God with all your heart and with all your soul and with all your mind."* Then He gives us a glimpse on self-respect because He says secondly, the next greatest commandment in **verse 39,** is *"Love your neighbor as yourself."*

How do you love yourself? He is assuming that we love ourselves. Maybe this is one of the reasons we have so much strife and division in our country right now because no one loves themselves. It is paramount to a healthy Christian life to have self-respect. To look inward and see God made you exactly how you are, and He doesn't make mistakes.

I have always been attracted to beautiful women. Both of my wife's were extremely beautiful women in their day, but both had self-respect problems. In growing up, my mother was key to that, and she would constantly tell me and my brothers that we were great and that she loved us.

Whenever she celebrated our birthdays, my mom would get the flag out and fly it. Then she told us that someday we would grow up and be president of this country. We all grew up confident and strong because of her. I have never suffered with self-image until my second wife left me. It was then that I was forced to take a hard look into what and who I thought I was.

I remember shopping alone late one night for food for the kids in Walmart. As I pushed my cart around, I started noticing the couples around me, typical Walmart shoppers, the ones everyone who thinks too highly of themselves make fun of, and I started to cry. They looked happy. They we together and I was so jealous. I remember thinking how lucky that husband was because he had a wife who loved him! She wasn't beautiful by the world standard, but she was at his side. She was a Holy wife.

In **1 Corinthians 3:16-17** it says, *"Don't you know that you yourselves are God's temple, and that the spirit of God dwells in you. If any man or woman destroys God's temple, God will destroy him or her, for the temple of God is holy."* And that is what you are, God's Temple!

Uncle Frank, my worldly mentor, again would say, "Give yourself a chance to win." You are Holy, get that in your heart and start acting like it! The Creator of all things made you just as He planned. We tend to look at the faults in others to compensate this most egregious character flaw when we fall victim to a poor self-image, and it manifests itself in a critical spirit towards others. Why do you think that God says for us to love our neighbor as ourselves, if we don't love ourselves first? When we accept Christ, we become sons and daughters of God through Christ (see **Galatians 3:26).**

I think it takes a fair amount of self-honesty to take stock in yourself in this area of one's life and Christian life. You need to go into serious prayer and ask the One who made you where you need help. Here are four basic steps we must consider when we take a reflective look at ourselves:

1. Realize your childhood environment does not have to determine your self-worth and self-respect. Forgive those who hurt you and give it to God. Let that anger and hatred go. It will only fester and weigh down your ability to recover the way God intends for you.

2. Realize you are a child of God, and you are allowed good things and happy feelings and give thanks for all the gifts you

have every single day of your life.

3. Realize you have needs. It's healthy to take care of yourself, and only then will you be effective in doing God's work.

4. Ask God to help you set healthy boundaries in the areas of your life that are affecting your self-respect whether it be people or addictions of various kinds.

LET'S PRAY...

Dear Heavenly Father of all life, I humbly come before You on my knees today with a heavy heart and a desire to repair the areas of my life that drive me into a place where I do not value myself like You value me. I ask You to help me answer these questions. Show me what I need to see about myself and how I got this way. Please, Lord, keep me from avoiding the truth. Help me see my inner fears on a daily basis and help me surrender them to You. Teach me what I really need to view myself correctly and then use me, Lord, in any way You see fit. Holy Spirit, rise up in me and show me the way to confidence and grace. Show me, Father, when I am being self-abusive and help me put that behind me so I can be more like Your Son who You sent to die on a cross for me. And it is in His Name, Jesus Christ, that I pray. **AMEN**

If you are suffering with self-respect issues, memorize this prayer and repeat it from your heart every morning!

CHAPTER EIGHT

Prayer and Secrets

What is a secret? I think we all know this. It is when we are entrusted with someone's confidence, and we agree to not violate it. A secret can also be something we deceptively hide from the world around us. Things we do that we don't want our friends and family to know about. I urge you to take a moment to think about the secrets you are keeping in your personal life and write them all down. We are going down a serious rabbit hole here and if you take an honest look down there you will see that the secrets you are keeping will seriously affect your prayers.

Why do we keep secrets from others? Is it different to keep secrets from men (women) and secrets from God? Well, if we think about this, the problem with secrets is they never stay that way! If you think that you can keep something quiet or that anyone else will keep your secrets, you're smoking crack. Secrets never stay secrets! And here is even a worse thought. If you think that you can keep something secret from God, the one who sees all things and knows your heart, then you're even more delusional.

Let's take a look at what might be some exceptions to this rule of life. In **Luke 8:17** it says, *"For nothing is hidden that shall not become evident nor anything secret that shall not become known and come to light."* Satan loves to tell us the opposite. He says, "You can do whatever you want, and no one will know." This is the opposite of this verse and a long standing lie from our spiritual enemy.

This should make you think. "What a chilling thought. Am I willing for everyone I know to know everything I do in secret?" or even worse, and more horrifying, "Am I willing for God and all His heavenly angels to watch me do the things that I do in secret?" Oh, these things we do in secret, how they affect the people we love and how they affect our Christian walk!

If you need negative motivation to clean up these areas of your life, then read **2 Corinthians 5:10,** which promises us all a day in the woodshed. For those of you unfamiliar with what that means, in the old days, backwoods country people used to take their kids to the woodshed for a spanking to punish them when they did wrong! God does the same with us. *"For we must all appear before the judgement seat of Christ, so that each of us may receive what is due us for the things done while in the body, whether good or bad."* There will be no hiding on that day!

Back when I was an atheist, my life motto was "Ultimately

Nothing Matters." This gave me comfort to do all the evil things I wanted to do because I believed when I died it didn't matter and I was only out for myself in those days. Now that I am a Christian and for the last 40 years, I have changed my thinking to "Ultimately Everything Matters"! Why? Because that is what the Bible says!

Ephesians 5:10-16 says, *"Trying to learn what is pleasing to the Lord, and do not participate in the unfruitful deeds of darkness but instead even expose them. For it is disgraceful even to speak of the things done in SECRET. But all things become visible when they are exposed by the light, for everything that becomes visible is light."*

Having a secret sin life will never end good. You must realize that and resist the thinking that you are getting away with anything for long. Also, I can tell you from experience, when I would go invisible and commit sin, the second I was done, I felt shame and wanted to escape the scene. Do you think this is how God wants to answer your prayers as you beg Him for forgiveness after you fall time after time? I doubt it.

In **James 5:16** this passage tells us how to start a healthy way out. Find a Christian brother or sister, a pastor or an elder and confess to them. *"Therefore, confess your sins to one another and pray for one another so that you may be healed. The effective prayer of a righteous man can accomplish much."* Christian community can be an awesome pain reliever and confessing your struggles puts you in a place to admit you need prayer.

All the prayer meetings I held in my home ended with all of us going around the room and asking for prayer from each other about the secret struggles in our lives. I saw strong men break down week after week, baring their souls to other men and an amazing spirit of grace from these men to each other as they prayed together for each man's struggle. You could cut the air with a knife it was so full of the Holy Spirit. Every eye would be tearing and every man in there was lifted up by the prayers of the group, and in the end, everyone would comment how relieved they were to share their secrets!

LET'S PRAY...

Lord of everything we know, You see everything both good and bad in our hearts. We know without a doubt that there truly are no secrets we can keep from Your eyes. We know that there will come a day when everything we have done in this life will be on the Imax screen on judgement day, both the good and the bad. Let us vow to move our hearts to live a life unashamed of what we do. No secret that hinders our prayers and the work You have for us to do. Give us the strength to resist Satan and his demons and help us not to invite them into half our life and You the other half. We know this is wrong and is an extremely compromising kind of life. Light and dark never mix, so keep us on the Holy path. **1 John 1:9** tells us that, *"if we confess our sins, You are faithful to forgive us and cleanse us from all unrighteousness."* So here and now, Lord, we confess our dirty secrets and unburden our hearts because we know, Lord, to follow You is a heart thing! We know You care and love us; we know You hear our prayers and how could this prayer be anything but Your will for us? Thank You, Lord, for giving me a heart and soul that loves You and wants to please You in every way. In my Savior Jesus' Holy and Perfect Name, I pray. **AMEN**

CHAPTER NINE

Prayer and Choices

Mathew 19:16-22 begins in a story of a rich young man coming to Jesus asking what he has to do to inherit the kingdom of God. *"And behold one came to him and said, 'Teacher, what one thing must I do to achieve eternal life?' And He said to him, 'Why are you asking me what is good? There is only one who is good, but if you wish to enter into life keep the commandments.' Then he said to him, 'Which ones?' And Jesus said, 'You shall not commit murder, you shall not commit adultery, you shall not steal, you should not bare false witness, honor your father and mother, and you shall love your neighbor as yourself.' Then he said to him, 'All these things I have kept. What am I still lacking?' Jesus said to him, 'If you wish to be acceptable to God, go sell all your possessions and give them to the poor, and you shall have treasure in heaven, and come follow me.' But when the young rich man* *heard this, he grieved and went away, for he was one who owned much property."*

Choices! Funny thing is you never hear about this guy again in the Bible. It is obvious he made the wrong choice. Those next verses go on to explain how hard it is for rich people to get into Heaven. Why? Because surrendering one's life and heart to God can cost you every earthly thing you have, and rich people do not like to part with their money, position, or power to control their situations. This rich man's heart was in his treasures and Jesus hit him where it counts.

Really, if you were face to face with Jesus Christ as He walked the earth in that time watching Him turn the world upside down, and He said to you, "Hey, do you want a free pass to Heaven? Go empty out, give all your stuff away and let's go perform some awesome miracles, and save millions of souls." Do you think you'd go, "Ahh, I'm not sure?"

If you look at the disciple's response as Jesus walked up on these hard-working professional fishermen who braved the sea daily to run their business, and He gave them the same offer, what did they do? They dropped everything—nets, boats, account receivable's, families, wives, and all—and followed! Choices, choices, choices! Life is full of choices. Probably one of the worst understatements ever written.

Let us ponder a serious question for minute. In the end, what defines our life here on earth? I read somewhere that the sum of the responses you have made toward God defines your life. Once God reveals Himself to you, the choices begin. Once the choices begin, then the responses begin. And after the responses begin, then the consequences begin! Once God reveals Himself to you, what is your next decision? "Do I follow Him or not?" Because we are all creatures of free will, that decision is ours to make! **2 Corinthians 5:17** says, *"Therefore, if any man is in Christ, he is a new creation. The old things have passed away, behold new things have come."*

We saw in previous chapters that **1 Corinthians 10:13** tells us when temptations overcome us, God gives us escape hatches and choices to make, just like the rich young guy and the disciples. We are presented with choices. Jesus spoke to both basically the same thing and there were two very different results. One followed and went all in, and the other chose not to and walked away sad.

If you are a Christian, then whenever Jesus speaks to your heart it requires an adjustment in life. If you are not Christian, and you think even remotely just a little that Jesus is talking to you and you turn your back and run, then you have chosen to live your life outside of God's will for you, and He will let you run into whatever trouble you want to destroy your life with.

Make no mistake, when Jesus speaks to you, it requires us to adjust our life immediately and follow His plan for us, no matter how crazy it looks to the world. Do you think the families and friends who watched the fishermen walk away from their rocking business, their homes, and families were standing there going, "Yea, you go guys!" Heck no! They were probably yelling at them to come back and stop this crazy behavior!

This truth drastically affects your prayer life. And again,

what is prayer? Our conversations with God. Our open, ongoing conversations and relationship with God. If He speaks to us and we are like, "Oh man, I hear you, bro but not now." Are we in sync or out of sync? And what is He doing when He answers your prayers? I believe He is revealing His will for your life. And then what happens? Choices! You have a decision to make: "Yes, Lord, I will do as You say," or you can choose to go Satan's way and turn your back on Jesus. Have you ever known anyone that seemed they were blessed by the devil?

I came to Reno not knowing a soul in the car business, and even though I had a monster history and a powerful resume, I could not land a General Manager job at any of the Reno or Carson City auto dealerships. We were running out of money and food, and my brother, who had been helping me, who's idea it was for me to move my family to Reno, was getting tired of supporting me. It's not that I wasn't qualified. It was that Reno had its own little mafia of car dealers and they didn't trust any outsiders to come run their businesses. So, I humbled myself and went on the line selling cars, and gradually I worked my way up the food chain in Reno.

Eventually, I got a 30k a month General Manager job working for a super wealthy Reno dealer who was so evil behind the scenes, I had a really hard time working for him and carrying out his business plans. He wreaked havoc on the customers and employees on a regular basis and was always fighting me to carry out his evil requests. It went against all of my Christian morals, and we fought constantly, and even though I had brought him to new levels of success, he demanded I do evil things. My Godly business ways were breaking all records and yet still he demanded I steal for him, cover his extra marital affairs with both women and men, and he demanded I rip off my crew of employees as well. Understand that this man was worth about 100 million already. He was truly blessed by the devil, and it seemed he was bullet proof in every vile thing he did!

One day we clashed for the last time, and I have to admit that I was scared to lose a 30k-a-month job in a small town like Reno. After all, this wasn't LA where I was from and well-known in the business, where there were literally thousands of car jobs to choose from, and virtually none like this in Reno.

My choice had come, as I bucked up to him for the last time and I knew when he walked out of my office that I was done. I chose not to follow evil no matter what the consequences were going to be. The next day he fired me, and I remember my wife giving me so much grief. She cried, "Why can't you just do what he wants? What are we going to do now?" We had been living high on the hog and hard times were ahead. I told her that God had always provided what we needed, and we would trust Him to continue that as long as I was faithful. She was furious!

The day he fired me, he gave me a $120,000 severance and $10,000 cash and told me he was sorry because I was one of the most talented car guys he had ever seen, but we just didn't see eye to eye. I didn't tell my wife about the money for several days because she had given me such a hard time for quitting for Godly reasons! I let her sweat it out (sorry, but I did).

Every day, God crosses your path with people He wants you to help, and every day you make choices. You can play church, or you can give Him your all. I read once in a daily devotional that your life is the sum of all the choices you make in response to God calling you. In the end everything matters, because God looks at the heart of men and women, and He wants to answer your prayers. The answers to your prayers follow your choices!

Just like when you read the Bible. If you read a verse and it hits your heart, you have a choice; absorb it and choose to obey or abort it and run. God does not need anything from us especially running around playing like we are good Christians going to church grudgingly for a couple of hours on Sunday, then hurrying off to go play. What He really wants from us is to rely on Him and not for Him to rely on us.

What did Peter, James and John do differently than the rich young ruler? They sold out and went all in. They left everything and followed! And how did that play out? Those men went on to turn the world upside down and started the greatest revolution ever in world history. The rich guy went away sad and was never heard from again.

Is God calling you in some way? Probably, if you're reading this book. What has your response been? Is it something like, "Ahh, let me figure out how far I want to take this 'Jesus' thing." Or "I trust You, Lord, I'm all in!"

Are you faced with the same reluctance the young, rich guy was faced with, that He's calling you and all you have to do now is figure out what adjustments you have to make, and how you think those decisions will affect your prayer life? Do you really think your prayers can be answered any other way? **Ephesians 2:10** says, *"For we are his workmanship, created in Christ Jesus, for good works, which God prepared beforehand that we should walk in them."* Are you walking in them? If not, maybe it's time!

LET'S PRAY...

Heavenly Father, help us to have the courage and bravery to make the right choices. Help us to understand that at any time our journey here can end, and we will not get more opportunities to go back and redo. Give us Your eyes to see the hurt in others that only You can heal and help us to share the great news of Your Son in their lives. Help us to be bold, and to choose wisely as we walk this earth, and to make You proud of us in everything we do, think, and speak! We know that everything matters, and we need the Holy Spirit You provide to spur us on to do Your will. Hear this prayer, O Lord, and grant us a heart like the disciples who walked straight into a life of obedience without any second thoughts! In the Precious Name of Jesus, I pray. **AMEN**

CHAPTER TEN

Prayer and Disappointment

As we develop as adults we are taught to strive for goals. We strive to get out of high school. Then some of us strive onward to get a college education, while others go to work, others start families, others join the military but, in some way, we all have dreams and goals as kids, and we want to follow those dreams.

We are driven by these goals, but when things don't go according to plan, we are disappointed. When plans fail, as they often do, we are faced with choices: Regroup and make a new plan. Settle for less, which isn't always satisfying. Or becoming completely derailed and starting over. Some things just seem to be out of our control and there is nothing we can do to change it. This is different than self-sabotage, but none the less, every bit as disappointing.

If you stop and look back on your life at any time, you will see the best laid plans of mice and men in progress! That phrase was written in a poem by a famous Scottish poet Robert Burns, and later into a book by John Steinbeck. The poem is about a farmer apologizing to a mouse for destroying his nest while plowing a field.

In the famous book, the concept is further expounded on when two characters' life goals are derailed, and plans destroyed. I know many times when I have worked insanely hard at accomplishing something yet never finished, and then I'd look at the situation and think in utter disappointment, "Stuff Happens".

If you're not a Christian and the world's goals are all you have to worry about and when disappointment overcomes, you can write it off to bad luck, karma or blame it on some person who caused the wrong thing to happen. But if you are a Christian, then you must look at how these setbacks effect your Spiritual life, assuming, of course, that you have Spiritual goals and you're not just floating along playing church. Some examples of Spiritual goals may be to read Scripture daily, tithe consistently, help others in need, attend church regularly (not just on Easter and Christmas), or even learn to pray properly.

What is the difference in being a Christian and not being one? Simply put, faith in God that no matter what happens to us in this life, God will use it for the greater good of His will for us. This is a huge realization and when you get this concept down it will change your prayers. To be disappointed itself is missing the purpose in the greater good. Disappointments in life can be paralyzing and turn us angry and bitter. When we solely focus on what we lost after we worked so hard, it's easy to fall apart and start down the wrong paths to further disappointments. Remember Uncle Frank's words of wisdom, "Give yourself a chance to win." But how do we do this?

We learn from the Scriptures that the greater good is always at work in a Christian's life. **Psalm 16:1-2** says, *Preserve me, O God, for in You I put my trust. O my soul, you have said to the Lord, "You are my Lord, my goodness is nothing apart from You."* David is crying out to God here to find a meaning to all the strife in his life and putting his faith in the greater good of God's plan for him. In other words, he is subjugating his goals and failures in life to God's will.

In **Philippians 3:8** we see the Apostle Paul realize this when he says, *"Yet indeed I also count all things loss for the excellence of the knowledge of Christ Jesus my Lord, for whom I have suffered the loss of all things and count them but rubbish in order that I may gain Christ."*

Wow, how many of us can say this? How many of us can say we have lost all things we strived for and count them but trash in comparison to Christ, or a true relationship with Christ? I'm thinking maybe none of us or, at best, just a few of us can say this because in today's world we are taught to cut our losses and save what we can. Then regroup and make new plans and get back on the road to success by the world's standards.

You see it in work, you see it in relationships and love, and you see it in anything frivolous that we pursue. But Paul is a perfect example of going all in and one who looked to the greater good of having a personal relationship with Jesus and considered it worth any suffering He had to endure!

God promises us that those who seek Him will lack no good. So, what is the greater good? Knowing Jesus and having a personal connection to Him is the greater good. Not just saying, "Yea, I believe in God," but actually asking Him to forgive you. Then acknowledging His death on the cross and ascension into Heaven and realizing He did all that to provide you a way back into the family of God. He secured your future as well as set your path here on earth. Do you know Him? God is the only all-satisfying good, which is why He is the greater good.

What truly makes something bad or good is if it brings you closer to Him. In **2 Corinthians 12:9-10,** Paul talks about his thorn in the flesh and answers to disappointments. *"And he has said to me, my grace is sufficient for you, for power is perfected in weakness, most gladly therefore, I will rather boast about my weakness that the power of Christ may dwell in me. Therefore, I am well content with weakness, with insults, with distresses, with persecutions, with difficulties for Christ's sake, for when I am weak then I am strong."*

So, if we look for the underlying reasons, and we are disappointed, we will see it's because we are seeking something more than Him or someone more than Him. It is a flaw in our faith because faith is believing in something you cannot see or prove.

So how do we start a new outlook on this ever-present challenge in life? For it seems that we will suffer many disappointments and it is so important to refocus our purpose on seeing things from God's perspective.

First, we need to come to Jesus with all our disappointments. We need to trust Him to meet us there and change our hearts. **Psalm 40 1-3** says, *"I waited patiently on the Lord, and he inclined to me, and heard my cry. He brought me up out of the pit of destruction out of the miry clay. And he set my feet upon a rock, making my footsteps firm. And he put a new song in my mouth, a song of praise to our God, many will see and fear and will trust in the Lord."*

In 2021, my brother and his wife lost their 31-year-old son to cancer. The community and all their friends got to see how a Christian couple deals with such a devastating event because both of them displayed complete faith in Tyler's death. Many were affected by their display of faith and frankly all our families witness during his passing was so glorifying to God that I know it had a long-lasting effect on the non-believers in our families' path.

If you find that the disappointments you are suffering are caused by the sin you have been committing, then confess them and reconnect to God again in a healthy way. **1 John 1:9** which I've quoted many times in this book, is your promise of cleansing and the first step in finding the greater good in hard times. Then you can pray for the work of the Spirit to change your heart.

The Spirit works through the Word so find Scripture and fight to trust the Word and continue praying over the Word until you feel the Spirit changing you in a deep way. Pray that every trial you suffer, that every disappointment you encounter will bring you closer to Christ. Look for the eternal purpose in all things. **2 Corinthians 4:17-18** says, *"For momentary, light afflictions producing for us an eternal weight of glory far beyond all comparison.*

While we look not to the things which are seen but as the things that are unseen, for the things that are seen are temporal, but the things that are unseen are eternal."

Pray that God will take care of everything you need in a way that will cause you to love and appreciate Him even more. Pray for everything you need, but fight to keep trusting Jesus as your all-satisfying treasure in life. Look for the greater good in all things in this life and you will sail through the hard times with a laugh of confidence and think to yourself, "The best laid plans of mice and men."

"No worries God, I will trust You to solve the hard times and focus on how I can be a light in a dark place for others to see and hopefully they will come to know the amazing grace that You show me and all those who love You from the heart!"

LET'S PRAY...

Master of Heaven and Earth and of all things created, hear my cries when I'm down. Help me to focus on You and the things to come, instead of being self-destructive. Help me to be a Light in this world and show my family and friends that You are real and that You care. Give me the strength to accept my beatings and smile in the confidence that Your love will bring me through all of this life for a greater Good. Give me the awareness to resist the evil one's small voice in my head that all is lost when I fail and help me to rise up and praise You in my walk through life. Thank You, Lord, because I know in my heart and in Your word that this is a prayer that You will answer. It is a prayer that is exactly in Your will. I pray this all in the Mighty Name of Jesus, Your Son.

CHAPTER ELEVEN

Prayer and Worry

All of us know someone that is constantly worrying about everything. The worry wort! Are you one of them? We can always find something to worry about. Webster's defines worry as: *To think about problems or fears, to feel or show fear and concern because you think something bad has happened or could happen: to make someone anxious or upset.* Bingo! So much to consider in this.

In today's society it has become an epidemic of massive proportions, so much so that we have developed a full complement of drugs that help society stop worrying. They are called anti-depressants! "Doctor, help me. My life is falling apart, and I'm worried about everything so much that I'm having trouble functioning!" Then the doctor complies, "Yea, I can see that. Let's get you started on some worry pills that will help level you out." And he gives you a six-month supply of Prozac or a steady dose of Zoloft. "And if this doesn't do it" he says, "maybe we can start combining several of these to fix your worries. Remember not to drink any alcohol or take any other drugs while you're on these. Let me know if things don't improve and we can try something else!"

The only problem is that all of these drugs come with a price. The side effects can be devastating. They can ruin your sex life, have weight gain, give you a feeling that nothing really matters, and for me, a complete detachment and lack of self-discipline. Yes, after my second wife left, I went on a depression and worry binge that was beyond who I was.

During a regular physical with my doctor, she says to me, "You look like death. What's going on?" I told her and, bam, I had the "cure"... Zoloft! I must admit it helped me to function better at work. Remember, I am a salesman by trade, and I'm forced to meet total and complete strangers every day and then convince them to spend thousands of dollars in a matter of a couple of hours. It's a hard thing to do even when you're in a great mood. But it's almost impossible when you are sad, depressed, or worried! Why? Because our emotions transfer in our communications with others.

When people go out shopping for cars, they are afraid they will make bad decisions, so they worry and put on a defense that they are not buying, they're just looking. But great salesmen know this is a front! When someone tells us this, what they really are saying is, "I haven't met the right salesman yet." But that guy or girl cannot be stuck in their own problems, or the customer will feel it and run. Sad people don't sell or buy anything in sad mode!

I was taught that everyone is in one of three states of mind at all times. Happy, sad, or mad, and people don't buy in sad or mad. Ironically people don't sell in sad or mad either. Only happy! So, the Zoloft was helping me get out of sad and into happy! Then some of the other salesmen at my dealership started to give me Vicodin as well to help me because for some reason this drug had helped them cope with the pressures of "full commission only" stress. I have to admit the "biscuits", as they are commonly called, worked great for me and I could sell like an animal when I was taking them daily.

At $5 a piece on the street, it was a cheap fix because when you're on straight commission it's like playing no limit poker. You can make whatever you're worth or go completely bust by standing out on that lot all day in the snow or 100-degree heat and not make a penny all day in a 12-hour shift… and the bills go on. If you start to string a few days together without selling, the worry becomes overwhelming, and the stress becomes crushing. I think I've gone seven days without selling and it's called a blank! A 7-day blank is like suicide time to a car salesman. That's half a pay period with no money coming in!

Anyway, I started on the Zoloft and Vicodin and began to sell again. Also, after eight years of not smoking cigarettes, at 60 years old, I started smoking again! My son Danny was living with me after he got out of a thirteen-month prison stint in California, and he saw right through my mess.

One night after work when I came home, he confronted me and said, "You're on something, Dad. Don't lie to me. I know it and maybe you don't see it, but I do." He busted me! Usually, it was the other way around. I busted him many times in the past, but it's definitely a wakeup call when your kid busts you! I admitted that I was taking about three Vicodin a day and on Zoloft too! The roles were reversed as he read me the riot act and I committed to stop the biscuits. That was no easy task as the drugs had their hooks in me and the guys at work started to offer them to me free just to help me out.

After my prescription ran out on the Zoloft, I decided to quit that, too, and just went cold turkey without looking into the side effects of doing that. I was having dizzy spells out on the lot and almost falling down at times when I was talking to customers. I was sick to my stomach for a week and miserable.

One day after about a week, I looked up how to quit Zoloft, and everything I googled said never do this cold turkey. I had done it and was not going back to wean myself off after I had tripped around for a week miserable.

The real point here is that I was a million miles away from my relationship with Christ at this point and was full of anxiety. I missed my wife that I still loved very much. The thought of her living with another man was killing me. I had moved from a General Manager job to the line selling cars so I could take care of my daughter Alese, who was 13 at the time and full of as much anxiety as I was. I was mean, even off the drugs, and I was struggling to make ends meet.

One day in church (yea, I went as so many people do as a secret agent Christian, sitting in the back and not talking to anyone, just listen.) That day the pastor preached a message to a full crowd of probably 500 people about worry and depression and feeling all alone. His words hit me so hard, I was crying in my seat. The people around me couldn't help but notice me wiping my constant flow of tears as sneaky as possible like real macho men do. But none of them approached me after it was over, so I tried to sneak out in the crowd.

I ran into a junior pastor on the way out (a complete stranger to me) and he saw me leaving with emotions all over my face. He stopped me, and said, "Good morning, I'm Pastor Jason Diaz. Are you okay?" The world stopped and I stood as people walked by all around us, and I poured my heart out to him. It was like no one else existed in that crowd.

The pastor listened and offered to pray with me and handed me his card. He told me to call him during the week and set up a meeting at his office so he could help me. He prayed a strong prayer over me, and I went to work on a Sunday. I was still very consumed with anxiety, straight commission, no help from my ex, bills mounting, kids to wake up and make lunches for, and pick them up after school. Dinners to cook, shopping for food, which I had never done before, laundry every night, homework to help with, and an empty, sleepless night staring at the ceiling in my empty bed thinking about her in another man's arms. It was too much.

The next week I met with the pastor, and it started a path back to Christ. I met another guy named Ryan who was studying to be a future pastor and I joined his community group. God had a greater plan for me, but at the time I couldn't see it coming because I was consumed with worry and anxiety.

Many things cause us to lose control; money, health, kids, sickness, marriages, jobs, retirement, politics, relationships, loneliness, being alone, people betraying us, and all of them cause us to worry. Then that worry turns into anxiety. Anxiety is when worry turns into perpetual worry.

As frail humans we run to the world's solutions by swallowing pills that our phycologists and secular counselors, or our family doctors who can write the scripts for the magic anti-depressants that are being consumed by millions today, but none of that fixes the real problem. Worrying about things you cannot control is like paying interest on a debt you never had. It's like sitting in a rocking chair and rocking; you're moving, but you're going nowhere.

Our sin nature and our evil helper in this world Satan, and he loves us to go down the rabbit hole of worry. He loves to mount up the pressure in our thoughts because he is the enemy of God, and anytime he can derail any of God's people, he is winning for a season.

So, let's look for a minute at what is the opposite of worry and anxiety: Simply put, the opposite of worry is Peace. The true cause of worry is the lack of faith. Think back into the Bible stories and look at a young, shepherd boy named David. As the field of battle lined up the brave warriors on both the Philistine and Hebrew side, they stared across the battlefield, when Goliath, a human freak of nature, a true giant beast, steps out and challenges any of the Hebrew soldiers to a one on one. He sends a mountain of fear into the warriors on the other side... the side of God, and they were terrified to go out and fight this guy so that their brothers in arms wouldn't have to die by the thousands, bleeding to death at hand-to-hand combat! Yet not one of them came forward to accept Goliath's challenge. No one, that is, except a teenage boy with only a sling shot and a stone.

David willingly walked out onto the battlefield to fight the giant because he trusted God and had faith when no one else did! After all, David had already killed a lion and a bear while tending his sheep in the past, and he knew God would see him through again... and He did! I have killed both a bear and a cougar, and it can be terrifying!

Faith: Think for a minute when the disciples were scared to death as their boat was about to perish in a storm in **Mark 4:37-41.** These men weren't amateurs. They were experienced lifetime professional fisherman out on the water everyday making a living off the sea, and no doubt had their share of storms. But this storm was a violent and they were panicking. And where is Jesus but asleep in the back of the boat?

These men finally get so desperate they decide to wake Him up and tell Him that they are all about to perish in the sea. And what does Jesus do? He looks at them, maybe even shakes His head and laughs to Himself. Then He calmly says to the sea, *"Be still!"* and the storm stops. Then He looks at His disciples and says, *"Why are you so afraid? Oh, you of little faith."* They were completely blown away and say to each other, *"Who is this man that even the wind and waves obey Him?"*

When I was studying the martial arts on my way to a black belt in Hwa Rang Do, I studied under the Supreme World Grand Master Dr Joo Bang Lee. This man could control his mind in such an acute way that I have personally seen him demonstrate feats of strength and superhuman unexplainable, mind-blowing things. Things like boil water in the palm of his hand, poke 16 penny nails through his hand, and when he removed them there was no evidence of holes or bleeding! He used to say, "You are not a true martial artist until you can change the direction of the wind!"

Jesus is a true martial artist if He can speak and calm the storms at sea. Peter learns it when he is sitting in chains in prison awaiting his execution the next day. He's singing songs of praise and not the least bit worried about anything when an earthquake happens, and angels appear to bust him out. The Apostle Paul who recounts being shipwrecked, beaten, starved, jailed, bitten by poisonous snakes, and a horrible of list of so much terror, and not once does he say he was worried!

You don't hear or read about the first martyr Steven falling apart as he was being stoned to death by the Hebrews, nor do you see our Savior worrying about His final death as He was being beaten and tortured by the Romans on His way to the cross. Go rent the movie "The Passion of Christ" and watch that again if you want a front row seat of how cruel the Romans were!

So why do we fall apart so easily? Worrying accomplishes **nothing** good. **Matthew 6:25-27** says, *"For this reason I say to you, do not be anxious for your life, as to what you shall eat or what you shall drink, nor for your body as to what you shall put on, Is not life more than food and the body more than clothing? Look at the birds of the air that they do not sew neither do they reap, nor gather into barns and yet your heavenly father feeds them. Are you not worth much more than they? And which one of you by being anxious can add a single cubit to his life span?"* Hello, Jesus is talking here!

So how does He tell us to fix this human condition we all struggle with? Go to **Matthew 6:33** and you will find the key that unlocks peace. *"But seek first the kingdom of God and his righteousness and all these things will be added to you."* Way to easy, right? Easy to read, easy to think about, but a hard one to grasp in real time! How do we do that?

As I have said all along, seeking Him is a "heart thing" and starts in your heart and soul. **Proverbs 3:5 says**, *"Trust in the Lord with all your heart; and do not lean on your own understanding. In all your ways acknowledge him, and he will make your paths straight."* Some real good qualifiers here when you stop to think about what is making you worry and anxious.

Have you or are you really ready to trust Him and let them go? Or maybe you are a stubborn one who likes to say to God, "Okay, God I believe in You, and I trust You in everything, except this one problem that I have to fix myself!" Sorry, but it don't work like that! That is not trusting with all your heart. "Give yourself a chance to win."

Read your Bible daily and absorb the Scriptures into your heart. Start gaining control through letting the Holy Spirit help you with your repetitive sin patterns that hinder your prayers. Give of yourself to others, give yourself time to listen to their problems and don't talk, but listen! Give of your finances to show God you appreciate His blessings.

Too many times I have, in faith, thrown in my last dollar at the time of giving and the next day a check from someone shows up in my mail or a customer would hand me a tip after selling them a car! Who does that? GOD!

Don't hoard! There is no need for it if you trust God. Birds don't hoard! Share Christ with the lost; make your stand public at work or with friends. You may be the last person they hear it from… you never know! Living like this will give you a freedom from worry and a peace that is uncommon among man! But most of all, learn to pray always, all day, every day. God wants to hear from you! He loves you and is studying your heart in all things!

Philippians 4:6-7 says, *"Be anxious for nothing, but in everything* (that means EVERYTHING) *by prayer and supplication with thanksgiving (that's means with your heart) let your requests be made known to God and the peace, which surpasses all comprehension shall guard your hearts and your minds in Christ Jesus."* Epic verses that cover everything you need to know on the subject of worry and anxiety!

LET'S PRAY...

Lord, we waste so much time in our lives worrying about petty things because we lack true faith in Your supreme power over all people and events in our lives. Help us, God, to see that our lives **are** Your concern, and that You **do** care about every little detail. Your word says that anxiety is a problem of faith, and we ask that You strengthen our beliefs and faith to take You at Your word because we know that You cannot lie! Our world is full of concern, and we need to refocus our hope on You through faith. The end result will be our testimony to others in need and we will be a shining example of Your children. Keep Satan far from us and break all generational curses that we could be under. Free us up to live happy and at peace with You in front of us, behind us, and at our side! There is no challenge we face bigger than You can handle for us. Let us believe it and live it daily. I thank You, God in the precious Name above all names, Jesus Christ! **AMEN**

CHAPTER TWELVE

Prayer and Anger

"Holy Michael, the Archangel, defend us in battle. Be our safeguard against the wickedness and snares of the devil. May God rebuke him, we humbly pray; and do you, O Prince of heavenly host, by the power of God, cast into hell Satan and all the evil spirits who wander through the world seeking the ruin of souls." Amen.

This prayer used to be repeated after every Catholic Mass up until 1964 when it was removed.

Is anger a sin? No. Sometimes we need to get angry to remedy a situation. Sometimes anger can spur us into action. Being angry is not a sin. The sin comes when anger controls us, and the situation gets away from our control. Being controlled by anger **is** a sin!

Ephesians 4:26-27 says, *"And do not sin by letting your anger control you. Do not let the sun go down on your anger, and do not give the devil an opportunity."* **Vs 26** comes from **Psalm 4:4** *"Don't sin by letting anger control you."*

Do you understand why there is this warning here? *"Do not give the devil an opportunity"?* In my humble opinion this is an insight on how Satan can access your thoughts and emotions when you are not guarding them and causes anger to become sin. How? When we lose our temper!

As disagreements and arguments quicken, so do the wrong things become said; which cause more wrong responses; which cause meaner things said. Eventually Satan wins! A full-blown fight of uncontrolled anger (maybe even violence) has come from a situation that could have had a peaceful solution and outcome if Satan hadn't prevailed in ramping it up!

There are a lot of great reasons not to lose your temper. **Psalm 37:8** says, *"Cease from anger and forsake wrath; Do not fret—it only causes harm."* Anger leads to evil doing. I guarantee that in my life it has led to saying things I regret the second they came out of my mouth! It has led to violence and being arrested and jailed! It has led to being physically hurt and injured to the point of hepatization and countless emergency room visits... even trips to the veterinarian.

Let me explain: When I worked for my uncle and when one of us got hurt while we were out hurting someone else (it was part of the job) and the police were investigating. They knew we got hurt and they would watch the hospitals and emergency rooms to see if we showed up there. But instead, we were taken to a vet in National City, CA, at any hour of the day or night. That old vet would patch us up and fix almost everything, from a bullet to stabbings, to setting bones. In fact, if he couldn't fix you, were probably going to die.

We all loved this guy and had confidence that he could fix anything! He would cuss and complain and lecture us, but never refused his services coming in the back door. I never found out what favor my uncle granted him, but this man patched us up many times and would never take money from any of us.

When we lose our temper, who do you think is in control? In other words, when you are out of control, who takes over? Satan and his demons! And what do you think their mission is? To make the worst possible outcome of any potentially bad situation possible! Why? It's their job to destroy souls, ruin lives, and take God's people out of service for God. So, I can tell you that we are the ones that can turn anger into a sin unless we use the greater power of the Holy Spirit!

As Christians, we have many good reasons not to let this happen. Even non-Christians have many good reasons not to let this happen, but they do not have the same resource we have. Prayer! If we learn to go to prayer **immediately** then we are invoking the Holy Spirit into the situation instead of the demons. If we learn to go to prayer immediately then our actions will be different, as will the outcome. If a bad situation hits you in the face and you pray from the start before you respond, then your prayers will be heard, and God will intervene. When a person is making us angry, and we want to lash out, it is going to cause a confrontation.

I used to be that guy, if you honked at me at a light or something, you had a fight on your hands. I don't know why that would instantly send me into a rage, but it did, and I would go out of my way to pay you back for being an idiot in your car. I'd slow down even more, or not move at all, or even at times, I'd get out of my car and confront you.

I have a huge truck nicknamed The Beast. It's a crew cab 4x4 long bed, diesel Ford with a big shell, and it's all set up for the hunting and off-road adventures that I love. This truck is the hardest thing to park anywhere and usually I have to back into most parking stalls. Amazingly, I can parallel park it in spots that others wouldn't ever try.

One morning I was running late to a doctor appointment, and I couldn't find a parking place. After searching, I found a spot on a curb and knew I could get into it. I started to back in sideways and the car behind me just lays on the horn, honking and honking for me to drive on and not park. I was about halfway into it when I lost my temper, and went to confront this jerk behind me.

I jumped out of my truck and quickly approached the car where I found a young teenage girl frantically rolling up her window. She was terrified that I was about to beat her to death. I had a few words with her that I'm not proud of and then got back in my truck and finished parking. She sped off scared to death. I felt so ashamed that I had lost my temper with that girl who looked like my 16-year-old daughter.

Another time in the same truck, I was sitting at a signal goofing around with the gear shift and accidently put it in reverse when the signal changed. I hit the gas and backed into the car behind me. The guy I hit gets out of the car with a huge hammer and starts to threaten me. He was screaming and yelling out of control. Other cars were just speeding away not wanting to get involved. I admitted to him that it was my fault and I apologized, but he wouldn't calm down long enough so that I could give him my insurance information. He was ready to swing the hammer at my head through the window.

I have a concealed weapon's permit, and I slowly took my 44 magnum from my briefcase without him seeing. I had a lethal repose ready as I continued to talk him down. I could tell he was high as a kite on meth, and I was a second away from killing him if that hammer was coming through my open window!

Eventually I prevailed to calm him down, and we pulled over to the side and I gave him all my info to get his car fixed. The repair costs were more than the car was worth, but I fixed it anyway. He never knew how close he came to being shot. And I would have been justified in shooting him, too (though I would not have felt good about it).

In both situations, as the aggressor and receiving the aggression, anger played a part in the outcome. I thought about how I must have looked just like that guy to that young girl and how embarrassed I would have been if someone had caught that scene on their cellphone and played it at church on Sunday for all my Christian friends to see!

The key to not letting your anger turn into sin is to focus on yourself first. You must instantly go to prayer in any situation and with any person who is making us angry. Pray for your heart to soften. Pray for forgiveness because we don't change people, God changes people, but how we respond can change outcomes! **Colossians 3:8** says, *"But now you yourselves are to put off all these: anger, wrath, malice, slander and abusive speech from your mouth."* Pretty simple, no exceptions here!

It goes on to say in **verses 12 and 13**, *"Therefore, as God's chosen people, holy and dearly loved, clothe yourselves with compassion, kindness, humility gentleness and patience. Bear with each other and forgive one another if any of you has a grievance against someone. Forgive as the Lord forgave you."* Learning to forgive is the key to controlling your anger. It takes practice to get good at it. Minute by minute, in the car lol. Hour by hour if you hate your boss. Day by day if your husband or wife is contentious, but it is possible if you are steadfast in prayer.

We pray and we forgive, and the next thing we do is love. Jesus said to love your enemies! No other options! *"But love your enemies and do good to them, and lend to them without expecting to get anything in return. Then your reward will be great, and you will be sons of the Most High, for he is kind to the ungrateful and wicked"* **(Luke 6:35)**. Wow!

We do not have the right to get our own pay back. Revenge and anger are not ours to use as Christians. Revenge and its wrath come from anger, and it has no place in our lives. Yes, you can get angry, and yes, you can use the anger to send you into prayer, but no, you cannot let the anger ruin your prayers, your relationship to God, or the witness around you!

One of the greatest Christian men I ever knew, Abe Rodriguez, was on his death bed with a terminal illness, and I drove all night from Reno to LA to see him one last time. I was trying to make him feel better and talk him up. My hope was that God would change things and he would be healed. Then Abe stopped me and said, "Tom, I'm ready. I have run my race. I have done what God sent me here to do. I accept the fact that soon I will pass, and I'm looking forward to finally seeing Jesus eye-to-eye." I was so moved and impressed with his faith.

Then he started to ask me about my ex-wife who I was still very angry with in my heart. I guess by my answers he could tell that, and he said to me, "Tom, God loves her, too. Why can't you see that she has so much value to God, and here you are stewing in it for what she did to you, instead of acting like the great Christian man God wants you to be?"

On his death bed my friend was still helping me be a better man of God just like he had always done for 40 years. Abe was one of the original men who took me under his wing when I first became a Christian and left the life of crime behind, and he was a gang member himself before God changed him! It hit me like a ton of bricks, and for the first time in my misery of divorce, I felt my heart change toward my ex-wife!

Abe passed soon after, but his compassion and love will never leave my heart. For God used him to help mold me into a man of service just like He can change any of you reading this. Anger uncontrolled will sideline you as a Christian and ruin your prayer life! Pray. Forgive and love!

Once I was tasked to settle a lawsuit that was being filed against a very rich and powerful dealer who I was working for in Reno. The guys working there before had sold an older woman a ½ ton truck to pull a camp trailer that she bought to take her grandkids camping. In essence they had knowingly sold her a truck that was unsafe to tow her travel trailer. To make matters even worse, she was completely buried and was sold this truck for thousands more than it was worth. They had compounded the situation by telling her it was safe and encouraged her to go try it. The dealership refused to take it back in trade and basically told her to pound sand.

The woman found a capable attorney and started a lawsuit to try and recover her losses. The dealer who I was working for was a super wealthy and powerful dealer in the region and had attorney resources that could not be matched. So, we all wound up in a settlement conference that had quickly gotten out of hand. The attorneys were saber rattling. The dealer was accusing the lady of being dishonest in her intentions, and the poor lady was being overwhelmed. I detached myself from all the arguing and just started to pray in the middle of the confusion. I asked God for wisdom to see the real problem and come up with a fair solution. He answered me, and I saw that all she wanted was to take her grandkids camping.

I waited for a break in the fighting and began to speak. I pointed out to all the parties that I believed the real problem was her inability to go camping and suggested that we trade her out of the heavy trailer she was in and put her into a half ton towable trailer. And to everyone's amazement, she instantly agreed, and the entire problem was resolved. The lawsuit was for a couple hundred thousand and God had just solved it for around $30,000. My dealer's high dollar attorney was amazed and asked me how I saw that. I told them all that I had prayed for God's wisdom during the fighting! They all laughed, and he said he might try that in the future. You can always depend on God to answer you if you truly believe He will, and if you go to Him instead of trying to go it alone.

LET'S PRAY...

Most High God, we fall on our knees today at Your feet and ask that You free us from all anger that has its root in the things or situations or people who have hurt us. We know that all things can be used for good if we let them, and we know that You are always faithful to be kind to us and forgive us everything we are guilty of. Help us to look at others as You do and help us to look at a lost world and see the opportunities that we have to help change others to know You. We can't change ourselves alone. We need Your heart in us. We want to live a life full of joy and thankfulness and focus on using the gifts You have given us. Hear our prayers, O Lord, and grant us the power of the Holy Spirit to learn to control our tempers, forgive others, and love our enemies. Thank You, Lord, in the Name above all names, Jesus Christ. **AMEN**

CHAPTER THIRTEEN

Prayer and Carrying Baggage

I often sit and ponder what is the biggest brick that I carry in my daily Christian walk from the past. I can look back on a 13-year life of crime, where I probably committed over 8000 felonies (a rough estimate), and many regretful things that still haunt my heart.

If you could identify the biggest brick that you carry in you emotional-past backpack, what would it be? For the purposes of this discussion, I am going to define emotional baggage as unresolved issues, either past or present. Things like negative emotions and feelings toward a person who hurt you, bad mindsets of unforgiveness even against yourself, hurt feelings, betrayals, bad treatment by work or bosses, rotten parents who could care less about you. And what do all these things have in common? PEOPLE! They are all events caused by people!

I can look back at two divorces, five kids effected by those divorces; I can look back even farther at my parents' divorce and how it ruined my teenage years; I can look back at stealing from car dealers who, at the time, I felt deserved it. Yes, at times in my life I've been a liar, a thief, a cheater, a violent force to deal with, and I've hurt many people. I've been a drug dealer and ruined many people's lives with that. I have caused and paid for many abortions in my rugged past, so I think it's safe to say that I can have a lot of guilt and emotional baggage if I sit down to think about it.

When I was 40, I was allowed into a rare and beautiful ceremony that had its roots in the Native American Indian custom of young men going through an ordeal to come through to manhood. In past generations, the young boys would be sent out alone into the wilderness without food or water. Just a simple spear or bow and they would have to prove their survival skills and warrior skills for a time. Then the tribe would accept them as a man and no longer a boy.

What I went to was a slant on that except we were going to deal with the emotional hurts of the past that affected us from becoming the men we were capable of becoming. I cannot give you the details of those five days as I was sworn to lifetime secrecy of the processes we were put through. However, I can tell you that it was an ordeal. We ate very little, if anything. We slept outside on ground. We were pushed physically, and we went to the sweat lodge for visions. The men who were going through it were all from different backgrounds and ages, and seemed to bond together as the weekend progressed. The leaders were rough on us, and we had to toughen up as the leaders within our groups began to surface. I had a lot of pride, and I wanted to be a leader of my group and so did another guy, and we were constantly butting heads in a mini power struggle.

As the torture progressed, I realized it wasn't that important to me as it was to him, and I backed off for the good of our group. One of the men running the ordeal took me aside and told me that I had actually showed true leadership quality by backing down, and it started me on a Spiritual journey to find out what baggage I was carrying that was affecting my growth as a man.

Eventually, each man, after being broken down for two days, had to enter a circle of all of us and let his deepest darkest secrets out. You had been brought to a place that was impossible to defend with typical macho-men behavior.

I volunteered to go first, and the leaders started in on me in the circle. Remember, I was a 40-year-old man with four kids, a great career, a solid relationship with Jesus, and had accomplished much. I was a black belt in one of the hardest martial arts in the world, and a retired race car driver who had traveled all over the world racing cars. There were also many hobbies that I had mastered, like deep-sea trophy fishing, big (dangerous) game hunting, and had fished successfully in the professional bass tournaments in Southern California. I had a twin-rated pilot license, and had briefly done a stint of sky diving. I was beyond blessed with a beautiful wife and, from all outside onlookers, it appeared that I was a really cool guy with many adventures and stories. In fact, I would not even tell half my stories because people just didn't believe them. lol.

But here I was in a Native, primitive, soul-bearing situation that there was no way out and no way to fake. As the grilling started, I had no idea what was going to come out of my mouth and when I broke, I started to cry and the words, "My dad left me at 13" nearly choked me. I bawled and bawled and never realized how much that effected my life because I was taught to man up and move on. I had been carrying that baggage for 27 years and it finally poured out of my soul in front of 30 men. I cannot tell you what happened next, but I will say after that session in the ring, I finally let it go!

I was amazed that of all the evil done to me in my life, that is what stuck in my way to true forgiveness and a peaceful soul. My dad and I were friends already we had a great relationship and I loved him, but I had never really forgiven him for deserting me as a kid.

I had made it through the ordeal and that night we danced to native drums around a big fire naked like something out of a "Dances with Wolves" movie, completely free of our worst baggage. It was a celebration of freedom.

Sometime later, my dad and I were on a hunting trip, and we were sitting high upon a mountain glassing at the country below when I shared my experience with him. He cried and asked me for my forgiveness and told me if he had it to do over again, he would not have deserted us. I felt so bad for him. We talked it all out, and we truly became close for the rest of his life.

I know that it is highly unlikely that any of you reading this will get the chance to experience what I did, but we **can** look to the Bible for the answers. The fact is people are going to hurt you and disappoint you and it is going to cause deep hurt feelings, and those negative emotions will affect your daily Christian walk.

In **Acts 20:23-24** the Apostle Paul tells us that once we become Christians, life is like a marathon. He is on his way to Jerusalem and certain capture and torture as he says, "...*except that the Holy Spirit solemnly testifies to me in every city, saying that chains and tribulations await me. But none of these things move me; nor do I count my life dear to myself, so that I may finish my race with joy, and the ministry which I received from the Lord Jesus, to testify to the gospel of the grace of God.*"

Our walk is compared to a marathon by him and guess what? Marathons are hard! You need to train to run a marathon. It takes conditioning running practice. You have to build up stamina to be able to run a marathon. It takes will power and mental toughness! So why do we want to try this epic run carrying a backpack full of bricks that will do nothing but weight us down and kill our ability to run the course that God has set out for us? What does it do to your performance? I argue that it will have a severe impact on training and your course. You will fail to perform at a peak level as God has intended.

So why do we make it so hard to drop the backpack of emotional bricks in life? Why can't we just drop it and run? I think it is because we deny the obvious; WE PRETEND ALL IS GOOD. That is what we are taught to do in the world. We blind ourselves to the issue because pride takes over and we don't want to admit weakness!

There was no hiding the night of that ordeal for me! There was no pride! It was all stripped away. The sad part of this is that we will turn to other destructive behaviors to cope with deep emotional hurts like, overeating, drug use, alcohol abuse, sex addictions, shopping addictions, become a work acholic and live in denial that we are carrying around a heavy load of bricks and trying to run! And the fact that none of this lightens the load, only creates bigger problems

So how does this common human condition affect your prayer life? When you are praying with a ton of baggage on your back it affects your heart. Your heart is confused, your mind is preoccupied, and you cannot get a sentence out in a prayer without losing your train of thought. How many times I start to pray, and a minute later I realize that I am not even praying anymore, but my mind has wondered off into total other thoughts that had nothing to do with my intended prayer.

The world chases a false doctrine of self-help. There are many life coaches and self-help gurus making millions on the human condition of carrying baggage from your past. But as with all things involving God, the answer is too simple! Give it **all** to God!

We have a choice in all things. He created us creatures of free will and we can run to self-help, or we can bury it and hide the truth in our backpacks, or we can fall on our knees and pour out our hurts to Him and decide to let them go! Fill up your life with stupid behaviors? Or let God in? Your choice.

John 15:5-7 says (and it's Jesus speaking), *"I am the vine; you are the branches. If you remain in me and I in you, you will bear much fruit; apart from me you can do nothing. If you do not remain in me, you are like a branch that is thrown away and withers; such branches are picked up and thrown into the fire and burned. If you remain in me and my words in you, ask whatever you wish, and it will be done for you."*

You cannot do anything when cut from the vine! That includes dropping the bricks. Jesus does not lie or exaggerate. He is God and He is showing us the key here to getting our prayers answered. **Psalm 33:4** says, *"For the word of the LORD is right and true; he is faithful in all he does."* He can be trusted! He is our healer, not some tv personality selling books! He is our healer in **Exodus 15:26**; He said, *"If you will listen carefully to the LORD your God and do what is right in his eyes, if you pay attention to his commands and keep all his decrees, I will not bring on you any of the diseases I brought on the Egyptians, for I am the LORD, who heals you."*

The way we let God in starts with prayer. It starts by starting a conversation with Him in total humbleness. We have a choice here; do we sit back and do nothing and try to ignore our heavy load as if it doesn't exist, or maybe you are a total procrastinator, and your game plan is to wait until just the right time? Maybe your heart is so hardened that you just choose not to believe in Him. I'm here to tell you that God can and will heal a broken heart. He can heal a wounded heart. He can restore your heart to a new condition and free you up to run the marathon without **any** baggage slowing you down.

So, make a plan of action to drop the bricks. Get on your knees in serious prayer and confess that you need His help. Read His word daily even if it's only a verse a day... start somewhere! Pray for wisdom and bravery to confront the hurt in your past from the people who let you down. Forgive them and reconnect with them and let them know. Let the world around you see a changed heart. It's a "heart thing" all the way!

John 15:16-17 says, *"You did not choose me, but I chose you and appointed you that you should go and bear fruit—fruit that will last—and so that whatever you ask in my name the Father will give you. This is my command that you love one another."*

Can you go bare fruit that has been weighted down with a hurtful past and you won't let go of? Are you following His command to love one another? If you harboring evil thoughts and hurt feelings on a family member, friend, or old boss? Maybe someone violated you sexually in your past, is that an exception? No! All the bricks will destroy your performance to run and bear lasting fruit, so let it go. Free your heart... pray yourself free!

In **3 John 1:2** it says, *"Beloved, I pray that you may prosper in all things and be in good health, just as your soul prospers."* Don't you see how it's all connected? Pray yourself free!

LET'S PRAY...

God of all things including our hearts and souls, I humbly ask from my knees that You help us to drop our heavy loads of emotional hurt, help us to forgive those that hurt us in our pasts in any way, and to focus on being the branches that You talked about bearing fruit, those branches that last for eternity with You in Heaven. Lord, hear our prayers and answer them in the mighty Name of Your Son, Jesus Christ. Help us to finish our course which can be harder for some than others, but if we acknowledge You in all things, You will provide the wisdom and bravery for us to let things go and serve You with happy hearts! **AMEN**

CHAPTER FOURTEEN

Prayer and Patience

Have you ever seen the cartoon drawing of two starving vultures sitting on top of a Saguaro cactus in middle of the desert looking like they are about to die, and the caption reads, "Patience my ass, let's go kill something!" How many of us are like that? It's a funny cartoon when you know that vultures do not kill things. They are not birds of prey. They circle the skies looking for dead animals to eat that other animals or people have killed. They clean up the scraps in nature.

God created vultures to be the bus boys and go clean up the messy tables from dinner when the restaurant closes. If you take a minute and think, really think, stop reading this after I give you this assignment and ponder and write down what the answer is because it is an important lesson.

What is the #1 thing you want to accomplish in this life?

Write this down, fold it up, and then tuck it into the back of this book for now. We will come back to it.

Did you think of it? Maybe it is relation based, like I want a husband and a family, or maybe you are money driven and want a lake house and money in the bank. Maybe you're climbing the corporate ladder and someday you want to be the big boss, and in charge of everything.

I'm a baby-boomer, and we were taught that to get what you want, you need to get out there and make things happen. No one is going to give you anything! Our parents lived through the great depression and starved on a regular basis. They fought the great wars and learned to sacrifice. Today it seems that the young people in general think they are owed an education, a job, and somehow, somewhere that work ethic seemed to slip away.

I know this is a generalization and that there are plenty of brilliant young people working hard for what they want, but the focus and training we went through is not the same today. I have hired many young people who want to start at the top and they think I'm doing them wrong when they aren't getting what they want by making them pay their dues. Paying your dues takes patience!

When we want things, we want them now, and most of the time we start asking God to grant our wishes like He is some sort of genie we can rub out of a bottle. And sometimes it happens, and I hear people just look in amazement and say, "OMG, it was such a God thing!" But honestly, if you live long enough, you're going to have to learn patience, and that takes learning how to wait! **ALL of life is supposed to be a "God thing!"**

I think the number one hardest thing we have to do in our Christian walk is learning how to wait. When you're not a Christian, you strive and rip and tear up the world around you to justify getting what you want the quickest way possible. But when you're a Christian, it isn't always in your control on when you get things! The difference being that if we really look at what happens when we are forced to wait on the Lord, we will see that waiting produces suffering! So, who likes to suffer, raise your hand?

I have been selling cars for over 50 years, and I have closed hundreds of thousands of car deals with people who should have waited, but they wanted what they wanted, and usually I helped them along that path. Occasionally you run into that one customer who is not controlled by their emotions and knows that maybe this isn't the smartest thing to do right now. They feel the need to wait, no matter how good I make the deal, they wait! And in the car business, this seems to be a great opportunity for everyone in the sales department to rag on you and tell you what a weak salesman you are for not closing that guy or girl... especially sales manager's bosses who will cowardly rip you apart for letting someone go when they were too cowardly to go out and talk to them.

It's human nature not to wait. It produces great anxiety! Going into a restaurant after Covid, you needed reservations to go out to breakfast a week ahead of time or it was a two-hour wait! Never mind, I'll wait two hours and go to dinner or lunch. Kids hate to wait naturally. "Dad can you help me with this problem?" "Yea, wait a second. I'm watching this game." "Come on, Dad, I need help right now!" "I know honey, but this is the Super Bowl!!"

How many single Christians, myself included, are tired of waiting for that "right" someone and decide that God doesn't care about them being single, so they go to the dating websites and compromise the heck out of themselves. I learned my lesson the hard way and gave up on all dating websites. I cannot seem to find one nice Christian lady who really fits her profile. It's funny in a way if it weren't so sad. Either her pictures are 20 years old and being a Christian to her means she went to church once 20 years ago, or she is a witch in stealth mode!

I recently met a woman who had all the greatest attributes. She seemed like a good catch, so we connected, and I set up a date for sushi. We went, and for the entire dinner she was lecturing me on how Jesus and Satan are best buddies, and she knows this because they were at a seance at the same table with her and she watched them hang out! I was horrified and couldn't even get a word in edgewise, and I can witness pretty good... but not that time.

To make it worse, the service at the restaurant was terrible that night and slow. It seemed that I could not get away to save my life! She kept wanting me to drink at dinner and was a great closer trying to take me home after dinner. She was attractive, and I had been celibate for a good amount of time, but she was convinced she could fix that. If you want to see how hard waiting can be, try committing to no sex in your life when you're single until you get married! I came home after and deleted my profile, and I prayed that God would forgive me. Then I asked Him to protect me from evil and vowed to be happily single until He decides that I'm worthy for Him to cross my path with the perfect girl for me. I was "scared straight"!

King David had to learn this the hard way and it is an epic study if you really dive into this guy. He had it all! Born in a faith that was uncommon among men, but like all of us, he sinned and made some major mistakes. Serious mistakes, like adultery and murder just to name a couple. But he had a heart for God, and when he was being hunted down like a dog through the desert, he had his coming to Jesus' moments and fell on his knees and begged for forgiveness and protection.

I urge you to stop reading this now and go read **Psalm 27**. Pay particular attention to the last two **verses 13-14,** *"I would have despaired unless I had believed that I would see the goodness of the Lord, in the land of the living. Wait for the Lord, be strong and let your heart take courage, and wait for the Lord."* When we look at the fact that waiting produces suffering, we wonder why God allows us to suffer so much. Like all great lessons from God, there is a greater purpose.

In **James 5:5-10,** where James is talking about misused riches, he puts things into perspective for us and gives us epic advice. *"You have lived luxuriously on the earth and led a life of wanton pleasure. You have fattened your hearts in a day of slaughter. You have condemned and put to death the righteous man; he does not resist. Be patient, therefore, brethren until the coming of the Lord. Behold the farmer waits for the precious produce of his soil, being patient about it, until it gets the early* *and late rains. You too be patient; strengthen your hearts, for the coming of the Lord is near. Do not complain, brethren, against one another, that you by yourselves may not be judged; behold, the Judge is standing right at the door. As an example, brethren of suffering and patience, take the prophets who spoke in the name of the Lord."*

Truth be told, it is not in our nature to wait. It is thought as weakness and it's hard to gain the discipline to wait. So how do we learn this skill? How do we cultivate patience? We do it with our hearts. We learn through prayer that waiting on the Lord to move on our life means learning how to endure the discomfort without complaining!

Look at **Proverbs 3:5-6,** a famous passage everyone likes to quote but few grasp. *"Trust in the Lord with all your heart, and do not lean on your own understanding, in all your ways acknowledge Him, and He will make your paths straight."* The key part of this Scripture is *"with all your heart."* Patience is a virtue talked about in 1000s of verses in the Bible, but in the end, being patient is a vital part of really trusting God!

So how does this effect your prayer life? The obvious answer is that if your heart is wrong, it will steer your prayers with the wrong motives. **Psalm 37:7-9** says, *"Rest in the Lord and wait patiently for Him; Do not fret because of him who prospers in his way, Because of the man who carries out wicked schemes. Cease from anger and forsake wrath; Do not fret; it leads only to evildoing. For the evildoers will be cut off, but those who wait for the Lord, they will inherit the land."*

How do we fix this and make sure our motives are aligned with God's so that we can have complete assurance that we can wait for His hand on our lives, and that our prayers are heard with a heavenly ear that will help us to endure the suffering without a heart full of hidden complaint?

One of the most valuable things you can do is a paradigm shift. In other words, instead of looking at the present when things aren't going your way, shift your thinking to being future focused. By understanding that God's timing and ours are not the same, we can learn to accept the fact we have to wait with a glad, non-complaining heart, to the future time that God has pre-ordained for us to see the lesson and outcomes He has designed.

In order to do this, we must learn how to pray for wisdom in our dissatisfaction! Learn to recognize the fever coming on and take some "prayer" Advil as soon as the temperature rises. If you struggle with this, I suggest that you dive deep into the subject and go look up all the verses that deal with patience and prayer. You will be amazed. Take baby steps!

You didn't get messed up overnight and chances are you're not going to fix it overnight! But if you really learn to trust Jesus, and not just give Him a cheap version of Christian lip service, then you will see that waiting with a Godly attitude is a trophy for all the world to see! And you can lay your head on your pillow every night with confidence knowing that you have become a weathered, mature Christian, not a whinny cry baby one... One who can see themselves in this verse. *"Yet those who wait for the Lord, will gain new strength; They will mount up with wings like eagles, they will run and not get tired, they will walk and not become weary"* **(Isaiah 40:31).**

In the last seven years that I had been selling Subaru's, I was, on many occasions, so fed up with the day-to-day grind and I wanted a job change so bad. I prayed that God would find me a management job, but every time an opening came up at Subaru, I was passed over for a young, up and coming sharp kid. I might have made the same decisions as most leaders are looking long term for young guys and girls that will stick it out for the future run. The timing was never right, and I had single-dad responsibilities that God had deemed more important!

Finally, when Alese had finished school and was out on the mission field, and my youngest son Cody was doing great after the Army and was working as a carpenter, I decided I wanted to take a year off and head to Baja, even though I didn't totally see how it could happen financially. The plan was to camp on the beach and write this book. I prayed about it, and right when I was about to pull the trigger, I got a management offer out of the blue! I would have to move, but it was only 180 miles from Reno and the job was an incredible opportunity.

After a very long seven years of praying in a miserable situation, it was a dream offer and I jumped on it. I had prayed my way through the misery (7 years' worth) with a glad heart and a knowledge that God would always meet my needs and that someday the suffering would end. And it finally did.

The real reason God sent me away from Reno was to write this book. I had procrastinated long enough and had continuously neglected the promptings of the Holy Spirit. So, I took the job and had to live in a trailer for a few months, and then in a mining camp for another few months. Yet I attacked this dealership with every ounce of experience and talent that I had. The funny thing was I had nothing to do in between or on my days off. I didn't know a soul because I was new to town, which was exactly how God wanted it, and all I did was write every morning before work and at night after work.

I laughed at God's sense of humor with me as I had a beautiful, comfortable home in Reno, but He answered my prayers by sending me to a rural mining town in northern Nevada called Winnemucca. I was lonely for friends and family, but I was making incredible money, saving it, paying off all my debts and, most importantly, I was finally writing again after a seven-year drought!

God had a different plan for me than Baja and I am happy that He worked it out this way. The downside of this story is that if anything goes wrong with this job, and it regularly does in the car business, then I am screwed because there are no other jobs in this town. Should I worry about that or just keep trusting God to know what is in my future? I think after all He has done for me in my life, I will just take it day by day and trust Him, "till the wheels fall off" as my daughter loves to say! He answers our prayers but teaching us patience along the way is part of becoming the person He wants us to be.

Okay, let us go back and get that paper you wrote your greatest desire on and take a different look at it. I'm sure there are as many different requests on it as there are people reading this. First ask yourself, does that thing have eternal Spiritual ramifications?

Or, is it something of this world? How bad do you want it? Are you more fixated on what that thing (or maybe person) can do for you? Will it change the way you feel about yourself or even maybe change the way others look at you?

A MOMENT OF TRUTH; maybe if you really honestly pray about it and empty all out to find a new strength in truly waiting on God **no matter the temporary suffering,** the epic truth might hit you in the mouth! That punch is the truth that God is the "Only Being" in the universe that knows the future and how your desires separates us from Him! Everything is His to give or take away. In Him is all wisdom, so let's all throw those papers in the fire and try something new. Start your prayers with a pure heart that you can learn to surrender your will to His will, and then be happy in the waiting as a true Spiritual Warrior, serving, not complaining.

LET'S PRAY...

God above all things, Creator of all things, hear our prayer for help this day. Help the ones who love You to have the courage to be happy in whatever situation, whatever station in life on this earth You have us in with a glad heart. We have so much in this life we take for granted and so many blessings around us that at times we grow blind to the blessings You have given us and focus on the wrong things. Lord, give us wisdom to be a future-focused Christian. Help us to learn to suffer without complaint in the world. Help us to grasp that You may have a better plan for us than we are planning, and that we will be so much better off trusting in Your timing. Forgive our dissatisfaction and strengthen our hearts to be a rock of faith and a witness to all who know us, that You are our God, and we trust You in every single little thing in our life. Hear this prayer, Lord. How can it not be Your will? Grant us the requests we ask, Lord. Protect us from the evil one and his evil army. Help us to mount up with wings of eagles, Lord and live a life with a happy heart worthy of Your sacrifice on the cross. In Jesus' Holy and Precious Name. **AMEN**

CHAPTER FIFTEEN

Prayer and Money

We all need money as it affects everyone's life in some way or another. We use money to pay our bills, pay our rent or house payments, buy nice cars, and travel. We bust our earthly butts every day to get the magic to happiness so that we can buy the things that make us happy! Or so we think!

Money is power, and power is such an addiction. I'm not going to address the non-Christ followers on this subject, only the Christians, for a very simple reason. I cannot assume for a minute that anyone who does not have the Holy Spirit living inside them and guiding them would be able to grasp what I'm about to write. The world is obsessed with money and all that it seemingly brings. To argue against it would be insanity for the unsaved.

If you want to find the ultimate resisters to the faith of

surrendering your heart to Jesus Christ, then go witness to the super wealthy! Of course, they will pay lip service to the cause. They might even write a check once in a while for a good cause, to help out and feel better about themselves, but they will not, for a New York second, want to release this part of control of their life.

I have made a myriad of car deals with wealthy people, and though I believe it is unfair to stereotype them, these people were, at times, some the most challenging customers I have ever had.

I've also dealt with some who were very gracious and even offered me large tips at times when I really needed it. But unfortunately, there were still those who would behave so greedy and biased that I just let them make decisions based on their greed and basically stopped trying to help them because I had no choice.

The worst deal I ever had was to a family friend, a man with a lot of financial resources who became so obnoxious and mean spirited that I literally had to throw him out of the dealership, and I refused to sell him a car. His wife and daughter were horrified and embarrassed by his actions. I must admit that he got me so angry that I let that anger take over, and I ended up lowering myself to his level. I did not expect to be treated so badly and completely disrespected by a so-called friend. Unfortunately, I was not a great example of a Christian businessman that day!

The difference in these two types of wealthy people was not Christianity because many of the really sweet ones were not believers. The difference was the way they perceived their money! Some had generous, giving hearts, and some were so obsessed with holding onto their money and power that they would grind you to death for every last penny. For them, money was a game that they must win at all costs! To others, being fair and allowing you to make a commission was a reward for doing them the same way.

The key ingredient was that I made it a practice to pray at the beginning of all negotiations with everyone I did business with and, for the most part, I can say that God always answered my prayers. I did not make everyone I helped a deal, but mostly for my part that wasn't the prayer! The prayer was for God to allow me to be His guy in the car business and be a good example of who He is in me. I not only asked God for wisdom and clarity but that I could help them to get the best deal I could, and for me to be able to make a little money as well.

I will work very hard for a person or family in need and, at times, even be under attack with my bosses for a family that God sends me who could use a break. You've heard it said that "money is the root of all evil" and to some degree this is true, but underlying that truism is not money itself, but a dark heart. I have worked for many car dealers that had so much wealth that their grandkids and great grandkids could not spend it all in three generations! And most of them were cursed in their family life and unbreakable sin patterns.

A study of lottery winners disclosed that 85% of them wished after 10 years that they had never won the money. Why? It destroyed their families, and the uncontrolled spending ability led them to misery. We strive for many things in this life, like good health, great relationships, perfect children, great careers that lead us to ideal retirement, but it's all a pipe dream without a greater purpose, and that purpose is a life in sync with the Lord Jesus Christ. None of these things will bring you true peace in this life alone… especially money!

I've known very rich men who were terminally ill with cancer and spent millions trying everything possible to get the cure. They flew all over the world trying every experimental drug and spending every last dime they had to stay alive. But, in the end, they couldn't buy it! I was with many of these men at the end of their lives sharing Jesus with them when they had no hope left, and thankfully most of them bowed their stubborn necks before it was too late! The truth is that Satan is at the root of all evil and he uses a twisted view of money to control a worldwide destruction of mankind. I don't have to tell you this as it is evident everywhere at all times!

When I was growing up, I used to hear my mom and dad fight over money and finances. We weren't poor by the world's standard, but they always struggled to make ends meet. I despised hearing those arguments as a kid and vowed to become a millionaire at a very young age. I was a born hustler and would constantly be starting businesses and, at times, my dad would come to me for a loan.

When I was ten years old, I started a trash can service where I went house to house before school and for 10 cents a can would take out their trash cans and then follow the trash man around and put the cans back in their yard after they were empty. This was in 1964 before plastic trash cans. Everyone had metal drums with funky little wheels welded on them and smaller old oil drums with no wheels. There were no plastic trash bags either, so it was a dirty job lifting heavy, smellie cans in and out of people's backyards. But I hit a niche and soon I was making almost as much as my dad was making driving a truck eight hours a day! Plus, I got a lot of tips when I went back to get paid after school. It was a cash business and I was paid in change, and I always had pockets full of change. Maybe that's why, even today, I can't resist saving my change or picking up a coin I see on the ground. Of course, it has to be heads-up, because salesmen are very superstitious.

Anyway, I was on my way to becoming a millionaire at ten years old, until I hurt my back one morning lifting too heavy of a can and couldn't finish my route. I went home and got my younger brother Frank and hired him to finish lifting all the cans. My first adventure having an employee, and Frank was always a difficult challenge. He blackmailed me for half, but I had no choice! The injury was serious, and I was out for several weeks and basically had to give the route over to Frank who quickly peeved everybody off and ruined the business.

I have been driven my whole life and until I became a Christian at 27, I had been running with all the wrong motives. After my dad left us, I started stealing and eventually selling weed in the late 60s. It was a new business and a fat one! That path took me into a career of crime at a young age and by my mid-20s, I was making thousands a week selling cocaine and high dollar weed. My front was cars, but my cash cow was drugs. The goal had been met. I had made my first million by the time I was 25 years old.

I had money spilling out of every pocket and was always a hair away from death or prison!

Like most drug dealers, I started to use the drugs I was selling, and my world began to crumble. I was being blessed by the devil and had escaped the attempts on my life and the police many times. I left my uncle's protection and was running solo, so I had no back up, and the constant flow of cocaine into my brain was causing me to get sloppy and very unhealthy. The money brought unbridled power and uncontrolled spending on things I chased that I thought made me happy... sex, guns (OMG an unbelievable amounts of high-grade military weapons), fancy cars, hi-tech radio devices that spied on the police frequencies, even the narc channels which I paid someone to get for me.

I had created my own prison, and I was beating on the bars daily to get out of a trap I had created for myself. I had a network of dealers who I trusted and who always paid me because they knew I was capable of extreme violence, so we didn't go there very often. I used the mafia connections I had in the LA mob that I grew up with in San Diego to do my dirty work and that took money! It was only a matter of time before my heart blew up or I got busted and, in that era, the amount of cocaine I was selling would get you 20 years in Federal prison where you did 80% of the time. But I had even prepaid the best drug attorney in LA fifty thousand dollars in case that happened, and I would send him coke by the wheelbarrow full whenever he asked.

Satan had me set up for the big fall and if you want the gory details of how that all ended, read my life story, "Crossroads

Untaken" in the book, "Dancing with the Scars2" by TJ Martini. This book you're reading now is a book on prayer, and I want to focus on how wrong motives in the area of money can easily ruin our prayers, and the converse concept that understanding how we should view money and its source will completely bless our lives and help us to live satisfied and in peace. It will also bless us as we move from this life into the next.

The world seeks money desperately and it's an easy mindset to fall in. Living in Nevada you will see new people who move here and become obsessed with the slot machines; mothers and housewives playing away their food money in the grocery store with their babies sitting next to the slots in a stroller. Meth addicts mesmerized by the spinning lights in every liquor and convenience store throwing away the change they stood out on the corners begging for all day; businessmen and judges and salesmen, because they are super compulsive people, betting sports with every dime they had.

The gambling promise of easy money is such a bear trap! But as Christians we are to have a changed heart. We are to look to God for everything and seek Him before anything! **Luke 12:15** says, *Then he said to them, "Beware, and be on your guard against every form of greed; for not even when one has an abundance does his life consist of his possessions."* Look into your hearts, brothers and sisters and search it. Is there a desire to make your life rich with anything money can buy? The revelation and secret to solving this problem is to look at the verses in **Matthew 6:31-33;** *"Do not worry then, saying, 'What shall we eat?' or 'What shall we drink?' or*

'What shall we wear?' For pagans run after all these things, and your heavenly Father knows that you need them. But seek first his kingdom and his righteousness, and all these things will be given to you as well." BAM! How do we miss this? How do we get redirected and blow this basic command to seek God and the Kingdom work He has for us to do, and get so self-consumed with what we are doing when it comes to money?

When I have fallen in this area it was because I had wrong motives in my heart. The Scripture says in **Psalm 34:10**, *"The lions may grow weak and hungry, but those who seek the Lord lack no good thing."* And in **Luke 12:48** it says, *"But the one who does not know and does things deserving punishment will be beaten with few blows. From everyone who has been given much, much will be demanded; and from the one who has been entrusted with much, much more will be asked."*

As modern-day Christians living in the USA, we have been given so much. I've seen the poorest people living in refugee camps go out and work for three dollars a day and generously throw what they have in the offering plates at church with a happy heart. Then I look around the rich churches in Reno and see obsessions with building huge buildings while the homeless starve for food and while the few Christian organizations like the Reno Gospel Center can't even get enough Christian volunteers to come cook and serve the poor 30 nights a month!

We have been given much and much is required of us, but there is a caveat; we must be giving with our hearts in the right condition. We must put our prayer life in check and make sure we are seeking Him first, from whom all blessings come, or again we will be praying worthless prayers that fall on deaf heavenly ears. The condition of your heart as it pertains to money and everything that surrounds money will affect your prayers.

Where do you stand with this? Are you giving enough? I read once if all the denominations members in the US faithfully tithed and the churches themselves weren't greedy and proactive in helping the poor in our country, there would be enough money to house and feed every homeless person, every family sleeping in a car, and every Veteran camped under a bridge in this country without the government's money! But no, we buy our houses and finance new furniture and obsess what kind of boats we need and worry and hoard for our golden years and then die as soon as we retire, and our kids fight for the scraps!

I truly believe that our prayers are hindered by the stewardship we prove out in our daily life. Once a month, the community group I led would go feed the homeless and there were times that I was broke and had to buy the food to cook for 150 homeless people, and it took my last dime. But here is a fact—neither me nor my kids ever went hungry, we never slept in a car, and we always had what we needed because God doesn't lie, and His promises are good!

Are you tithing? Are you investing in things with eternal consequences? Remember, you can't take it with you when you die. There is never a time when you will see a hearse pulling a U-Haul trailer to a funeral. Are you helping the needy around you? Look around! They are everywhere! Single moms struggle working jobs all day or night and then work all their days off taking care unselfishly of their children. Can you put an anonymous gift in their mailbox? Do you have a hoard of clothes and shoes sitting in your closet that you don't wear, when it could bring comfort and warmth to someone who can't afford to shop anywhere except The Good Will, if even that?

Are there cupboards of blankets and linens in your house that sit there 365 days a year while the poor freeze? What kind of example are you setting for your children? Your teenagers seek the quick buck because they worship a culture of instant millionaire rappers or drug-selling gang thugs. We wonder why the teen suicide rates are skyrocketing while the parents drive their Porsches and Teslas around to church looking cool and getting right back into hustling after our 90-minute dose of religion on Sunday.

If this sounds too familiar, ask God to forgive your heart and pray for wisdom in this critical area of your life. Get organized and dedicate your finances to Him. After all, it comes from Him! If He decides you need a spanking and takes it all away from you by you losing your business, or a job, or a sickness that stops your hustle, see how fast your fair-weather friends disappear and see who is left standing to pick you up. It will be Him again from who all good things come!

Pray about every decision and realize Who and what you are working for. Open your eyes to see where and in what areas of your life you are not living like He has planned for you, causing you to waste His blessings. Make small changes at a time. These things did not get this way overnight and most likely they will not get fixed instantly.

Once you have the proper perspective, start a Godly plan, and give generously. Smile at hard times because God is in control, and He knows without a doubt what you need. He is intently looking at your heart when you pray. Ask Him how you can use the gifts He has given you and the money He has entrusted you with to serve His purposes in your life. Do this and your prayers will be answered because they will align naturally with His plan for you. Fight this and you will never have enough to make you happy and you will be praying like a beggar not His heir!

LET'S PRAY...

Most High God of everything seen and unseen, we fall on our knees this moment and ask for forgiveness in the area of money and how we have missed the big picture that You have for us. We ask in a mighty and confident way for wisdom and eyes to see the plan You have for us, and to use the gifts and the money You enable us to make to further Your kingdom while we are here on Earth. We ask that You give us generous hearts who give without a need for recognition from anyone but You. Our reward is in Heaven, our riches we seek to store up in Heaven instead of here where it is guaranteed to rot. Help us, Lord, to have a heart that honors You and give us the stamina to live this life as an example to our children, our friends, our coworkers and even to poor strangers who, as You have said in Your words, might be angels in disguise. Thank You, Jesus, for all of our blessings and help us to be good stewards of all You give us! **AMEN**

CHAPTER SIXTEEN

Prayer and The Past

Living in the past has a huge effect on how we see the world around us and consequently effects our prayers in many ways. Think about this fact for a minute, and compare your past to someone who appears to have had a perfect past? I would wager there is no such person.

As people who are influenced minute by minute of the world view, we are bombarded with messages that we are victims of everything, especially our past. We are taught the things that happened to us that were unfair or unjust gives us the right to walk around either with a huge chip on our shoulder wanting a fight, or that it's okay to feel sorry for ourselves and self-medicate in anger.

If you were deserted, neglected, or abused as a child, you may feel that you have the right to be mad and claim insanity in your current life. In my case, it caused me to rebel against God and completely deny His existence for over 14 years. That rebellion developed me into a money-motivated criminal in my youth that in those 14 years, committed close to 8000 felonies, served jail time, hurt too many people, and had paid for abortions.

I also know where all the bodies are secretly and silently buried; I know where all the instruments of death are, and how they were destroyed; I know and live with all these terrible memories of my past, but I can honestly tell you now that it doesn't affect my daily life any longer.

All of us have things in our past we would like to forget. Unfortunately, do-overs are not an option. We cannot reverse the past from our minds, and if we don't get this into its proper perspective, it can eat us alive from the inside out like a parasite that cannot be identified. Yes, the past we share that is indelibly inked in our memory can and will affect our future, **if we let it**.

The world's opinion that we are beaten over the head with is simple, and it's a lie for those who accept Jesus into their lives. That lie is simple and absolute, "If you were hurt along the way on life's journey then your future will struggle with your past! It can lead you into addictions, divorce, prison, financial ruin, starvation, homelessness, sex abuse and, in extreme cases, even suicide."

Some bad people even like to brag about all the bad things they have done to justify their wickedness by blaming it on their past! The root of this is sin, and one unshakable fact is that we are living in a sinful world and sin is going to happen to us! It's a sure thing because we were all born sinners! But as Christians we are forgiven and are supposed to beat to a different drum once that happens. Forgiveness has a multifaceted purpose that sometimes we miss. Not only are we to forgive those who hurt us, but even more so, we are to forgive ourselves!

It is an important fact that so many of us miss... that if God has truly forgiven us (and He always does **when** we ask Him), then why are we so hell-bent on holding onto our past sin guilt? By doing this we will surely miss the purpose that God has for our life, and instead focus on the hurt we caused or the hurt that was done to us. Either way, it will cause us to have a heart that is clouded and not seeking God first above all things, which consequently will hinder our prayer life.

The secret to freedom from our past is in **2 Corinthians 5:17-21:** *"Therefore, if anyone is in Christ, he is a new creature; the old things passed away; behold, new things have come. Now all these things passed away; behold, new things have come. Now all these things are from God, who reconciled us to Himself through Christ and gave us the ministry of reconciliation, namely that God was in Christ reconciling the world to Himself, not counting their trespasses against them, and He has committed to us the word of reconciliation. Therefore, we are ambassadors for Christ, as though God were making an appeal through us; we beg you on behalf of Christ, to be reconciled to God. He made Him who knew no sin to be sin on our behalf, that we might become the righteousness of God to Him."*

When was the last time you were begged by someone like the

Apostle Paul? Go back and take a minute to really absorb this verse, and then give a valid excuse to go around moping about your past! Does that mean we are to forget the past—absolutely not! An ambassador is picked by kings to go out into foreign places and use the wisdom from their past to make relationships with strangers. To create bridges that different people can cross and learn from each other.

Think for a second if Jesus thought like this, He could justify sending any of us to Hell because our sin caused Him to have to leave Heaven go to Earth, taking on human form, experiencing a poor life, taking up carpentry, and eventually being killed by the hand of evil men... the most horrible death imaginable at that time. We look at that and think to ourselves, "Yea, I'm going to dwell on my miserable past before I can acknowledge the unselfish act that Jesus did for me!" Really? How's that working out for you? I hope with all hope that time here on Earth doesn't run out for you before you wind up on your knees.

The alternative decision is to realize that God has a purpose for you while you are here as His ambassador. Such an important title, but it comes with important duties. To accept Christ means to go to work using your past and everything you know, and go out and spread the Word of Grace and Reconciliation to all those you know or come in contact with. We don't forget the past; but we don't live in it either. We look to the future in freedom.

Once you are saved, God doesn't see your past any longer, for you are covered by the blood sacrifice of Christ. So, if He isn't holding your past against you, why should you hold your past against yourself? **Isaiah 43:25** says, *"I, even I, am the one who wipes out your transgressions for My own sake, and I will not remember your sins."* So why should we give our past center stage in our hearts? To do this means that we are motivated by it in a negative and destructive way. There is no peace being motivated by the past. Instead, we must find our hope and motivation by looking to the future. We look to the future with hope and a purpose! The world will say, "Look what I have become and look what I had to overcome with the past I had." But the Christian will say, "Look what I am becoming with the Holy Spirit in my life." Two very different points of view. The proverbial "different drum."

Christians know the future is bright. They know that God has their backs and someday they will stand and look Christ in the eyes in person, and they will spend eternity with Him. Christians already have the advantage, by faith, to know how all this crazy world ends and how Satan is going down. They know that all the injustices will be righted, no matter what horrible stuff they've done or that has been done to them. They have work to do here!

Are you preoccupied with the past? Then pray! Right now! Pray for God to open your eyes to the future that awaits you. Take a look into the heart of Paul when he says in **Philippians 3:13-14,** *"Brethren, I do not regard myself as having laid hold of it yet; but one thing I do: forgetting what lies behind and reaching forward to what lies ahead. I press on toward the goal for the prize of the upward call of God in Christ Jesus."* This coming from a man who hunted down Christians and stood by while they were killed or imprisoned! A man who left his past behind to become the greatest ambassador the world has ever experienced! Essentially, Paul says to let the past go and press on with the future.

Pray for forgiveness of your past, and yes and thank God that He forgives you and doesn't hold it against you. Then forgive yourself and be future focused. He wants you in the game because you got skin in the game! So, press on my friends and use the gifts you've been given; use the stripes you earned by surviving your past to get the work done that God has planned for you!

1 Corinthians 1:18 says, *"For the word of the cross is foolishness to those who are perishing, but to us who are being saved it is the power of God."* Satan is the great deceiver and once you're in the game, all in, even he will disguise himself as a vision of light to destroy your work in Christ. **2 Corinthians 11:14** says, *"And no wonder, for even Satan disguises himself as an angel of light."*

How many cherished family members do you have who are not saved? How many great friends do you have who are perishing if the clock stops ticking for them today? How many strangers has God sent you, but you missed the opportunity to pray for because you didn't ask? You are called to be an ambassador, so for Heaven's sake, act like one! Do it with a brave heart and future-focused attitude. Do it out of a supernatural love that only the Holy Spirit can provide you with. And above all things, move on from the hurt of the past.

Recently I spoke at the funeral of my step grandson who was shot to death in LA by gang members as he sat in his car minding his own business. He was mistaken as a gang enemy and consequently murdered as he was in the wrong place at the wrong time! The funeral was held on his 21st birthday and, needless to say, it was an emotional event. So young, with so much future ahead of him. He was just starting to develop into a great young man.

This was a tragedy that caused everyone to think of the unfairness of life. Yet, at the same time, it was an opportunity for the family to share their faith in Christ to those around the scene. His name was Isaiah and thank God he was saved. Isaiah had come hunting with me once in the mountains of Northern Nevada and, being a city kid, was blown away by the wilderness experience. He cried when he had to leave me and told me he wished he could stay! Now I look back to that moment in time and see just how precious those tears were.

We never know when the last time could be when we see someone here on this earth. You have a call, and it is a serious one because God is waiting on the line for you to pick up! Life is all about making choices, and the success of your life is determined by the sum of all the choices you make toward God! So, for Heaven's sake, pick up the proverbial phone and get in the game!

LET'S PRAY...

Precious God and Father of all Creation, thank You for giving to me a new seriousness of what is important to You and not following the wrong paths seeking the things of this world, but sharing Your love with lost and hurting people around me. Help me to be grateful for all the little things You provide and protect me from the evil one and his wretched army of evil helpers that You allowed me to fall into in my past and survive! Thank You that through the blood of Your Son I am forgiven and not held accountable for my past. Help me to forgive myself and all those who hurt me along the way. Lord give me the courage to answer Your call and use my past life experiences to serve as an ambassador of reconciliation. Make me an effective servant, Lord, in all ways. I am forever grateful. In Jesus' Holy and precious name. **AMEN**

CHAPTER SEVENTEEN

Prayer and The Future

We looked in the previous chapter how prayer can change our perspective of the past and free us up to serve God and live productive lives not being dragged down by the past. God does not want this kind of life for us. Instead, He wants us to be future-focused, keeping our attention on the things to come. It's like driving a car and constantly looking in the rear view instead of where you're going. That is a dangerous habit, not only while driving, but in life!

For the past six years, I have been guiding big game hunters and helping to teach people how to survive in the outdoors. Navigating the wilderness is an essential skill if you want to get back alive. I can't tell you how many people who don't practice the outdoors that cannot find their way back to the truck. I have experimented many times with novice hunters letting them try and guide us back, and usually they cannot. The reason is that they are focusing on where they've been, constantly looking back to find their way forward. Novice hikers and hunters get lost all the time following where they think they've been.

One time when I was a young hunter in my 20s, I was hunting black tailed deer in the Sierra Nevada mountains, and I spotted a big buck and began to track him all day. The stalk lasted hours but I never got a shot at him. When I started to go back, I tried to follow my tracks out, but everything looked different, and soon I was completely confused. A panic sets in when it's getting dark, and you are lost in the woods. The reality of spending the night alone and cold is a scary thing when you're not prepared for it or experienced at it.

I kept trying to find my way out, but my confidence level was quickly melting away. I was camping and hunting with three older friends who were experienced outdoorsmen, and I was going to be really embarrassed if they had to come find me. Darkness was setting in at rapid speed, and finally I gave up. I found a nice place to lay under a good tree for shelter and gathered a night's worth of firewood and then settled in to spend the night. I had sense enough to know that tripping around in the dark forest without a flashlight was not a good thing to do.

I had walked at least a mile or two toward the direction of the logging road I had left from when I started to go after the deer, but absolutely nothing looked familiar. I lost my tracks, and I was shook-up. I didn't have a day pack loaded with all the emergency supplies you need to be secure and comfortable for a night in the woods. I was kicking myself in the butt and about to light my fire and spend a very long night freezing outside when suddenly, I hear a truck coming. You can hear vehicles for miles in the mountains and desert, and I'm like, "What the heck?" It was coming closer as it bounced over the rocky trail. I grabbed my rifle and started moving in that direction in the dark, and suddenly I see head lights just 50 yards from me. It was my friends who were out looking for me!

I ran to the road and jumped in not telling them that minutes before, I was preparing to sleep under a tree! The funny part is I was only 50 yards from the road that I was looking for but couldn't see it from where I was. I was so thankful to see them.

One of them, Dennis Didieu, a SOG warrior from Vietnam war, knew I was lost and when we got back to camp, he gave me a good talking to about being prepared. The next day he took me hunting and taught me how to navigate, marking major landmarks instead of following my past. It's a skill I have been working on for the last 40 years now and have passed onto many up-and-coming outdoors people.

Our prayer life is very similar; you can get lost on your prayer path by not navigating it properly. God wants us to be future focused and moving forward at all times. **Proverbs 4:25-26** says, *"Let your eyes look directly ahead and let your gaze be fixed straight in front of you. Watch the path of your feet and all your ways will be established."*

What happens when we accept Christ? We become new

creatures. We ask for forgiveness in our confessions. And we are forgiven and receive the Holy Spirit, and a cleansing overcomes our souls! **Romans 10:9-10** says, *"If you confess with your mouth that Jesus is Lord, and believe in your heart that God raised Him from the dead, you will be saved; for with the heart a person believes, resulting in righteousness, and with the mouth he confesses, resulting in salvation."* So simple and yet so many Christians and churches today like to complicate this!

After that epic change, our life's communication with Him opens up in the form of prayer and He wants us to focus on the future... not the past! The Apostle Paul in his letter to the Philippian church says in **Philippians 3:13-14**, *"Brethren, I do not regard myself as having laid hold of it yet; but one thing I do: forgetting what lies behind and reaching to what lies ahead. I press on toward the goal for the prize of the upward calling of God in Christ Jesus."*

As natural humans we worry about all the wrong things in our future instead of pressing on like the Apostle Paul shows us. Things like money, houses, sickness, retirement, kids' future, jobs, who we are going to find to marry and have a family with when we are young or (like me) even who we are going to find to marry after we are old and divorced?

We become racked with fear, and we run to things and to the wrong people. The wrong ideas and solutions can go on for days, weeks, and even years... years upon years of constantly being lost in the woods, our confidence shattered, just like I was that day years ago. But here is some good news from **John 14:27**, straight from the words of Jesus as He was about to ascend back into heaven. *"Peace I leave to you, My peace I give to you; not as the world gives do I give to you. Let not let your heart be troubled nor let it be fearful."*

So how should we look at our future? We should look to the future with a supernatural hope that covers all our needs and wants down here. We should strive to align our daily lives with the things God has planned for us instead of the false hopes of the world.

In **1 Thessalonians 5:16-18** it says, *"Rejoice always, pray without creasing, in everything give thanks; for this is God's will for you in Christ Jesus."* Bingo! Why are you here? What kind of future do you want for yourself and your family? What are you going to do from here to change it? How far are you willing to go toward God to align yourself and your future to His plan for you?

It takes a complete "sell out" to move to the next level of faith! Read your Bible daily and communicate with Him always! Pray without stopping, get involved in a Christian community, go to church, seek strength and wisdom to defeat your sin patterns (whatever they are), speak up to hurting people around you, make your stand public, wear a cross to show who you are, and give generously to prove your confidence in God by not hoarding the things of this world. Share your hope in Christ with the lost and get in the war against Satan by going all in and making a point to become a mature Christian who walks with purpose!

Or you can take the other route and just "play" church, hitting a Bible study once in a while, because you're too busy right now. "I'll catch up on all this God stuff in the future." But your future may be shorter than you think. Don't wait! The future is now! Go back to **1 Thessalonians 5:2**, *"For you yourselves know full well that the day of the Lord will come just like a thief in the night."* If you're not ready, you won't have time to prepare. God wants you to be future-focused right now, and your prayer life can change your future!

LET'S PRAY...

Lord in Heaven, give us the mindset to leave the worry of this world behind us in our daily lives and help us to focus on You and what You have planned for us in the future. It's so easy to get lost in the things of this world that we miss the big picture of how much You love us and how much You desire to meet all our needs here. Help us to be future focused and strive to become the genuine real-deal kind of people here who can make a difference with our friends and family. Give us the wisdom to look at our major landmarks as we hike in this life and keep us from getting hopelessly lost! Give us courage not to wait, but to learn to navigate this life through constant righteous prayer. Setting our feet on Your path as You guide our steps! In Christ Holy name, I pray. **AMEN**

CHAPTER EIGHTEEN

Prayer and The Big Picture

As you look at yourself and think to the way you are today, is there that one person in your family or even a friend who God used in a powerful way in your life? If you are a non-Christian, a believer in randomness, then you can look back at that person and just think that you were lucky to have had them around. But if you are a believer in God and His order of things then it is fair to ask the question, "How do I fit into this grand scheme of things?" The proverbial big picture!

When we take a serious look at the big picture, we can see that too much has gone on before us for everything just to be happenstance. There are those people who can naturally look at situations in life and grasp the whole scene looking for a better understanding of things based on a view that an eagle would have from way above the ground? Then there are people who, for whatever reason, can only focus on themselves in their petty world and can't seem to get out of their own way to make something positive out of life.

We are all dealt some bad cards in the poker game of life. But it's how you view the game, not the hand, that determines how God can use you! God always speaks to us in a context of what He has done in the lives of those who have come before us. Think back in your family history and remember that one person who He used in your life to help mold you into someone who could make a difference to those you are older than now. Who was that person? For me it was my Arabic grandmother, a woman so spectacular in love that I have probably thought of her 10 million times since her early death in 1973.

My grandmother was born into this world as Della Saloom. She was a Syrian and was actually born a US citizen in this country in the late 1800's. Her father, in an effort to escape the poverty of 19th century Syria, moved his family of five boys and a wife to the United States because one of his brothers had come to New York and written him letters of how great it was here.

The trip was arduous in those days as you would have to go by horse and wagon to Palestine, then take a boat to Paris, then wait for a transatlantic boat to take the entire family to New York. He had to work along the way to feed them all. No easy journey by any standard with an entire family of five young boys in the late 1800's. They made it and hit this country in the winter of 1899.

My grandmother was born in 1900, in the USA. As the story

goes, my great grandfather did not like it here and missed the old country, so he decided to move them all back to Damascus. They resettled somewhere close to the Armenians, and in 1915, the Turkish Ottoman empire slaughtered thousands of innocent civilians and her family was caught up in the genocide. Her father was killed by the Turks defending his family, and her mother was captured, raped, and drug to death by Turkish soldiers and was tied to a war horse and drug through the streets of the town where they lived. Her brothers escaped carrying my grandmother along as she was a small, young teenager probably 15 years old. The remaining family took the older boys, but none of them wanted a girl because girls were second-class citizens and considered a burden.

My grandmother was given to a Christian orphanage in Beirut to be raised. There she was introduced to Jesus Christ and received schooling to become a nurse. She thrived alone with no close family, but she told me the people in the orphanage always treated her good and she was grateful for her life. As a young woman she became a Christian and worked in the hospital and lived in the orphanage helping to care for the younger orphans that came after her.

One day she met a handsome young man who came from a rich and prominent family that had resettled from Palestine to Beirut. His name was Saba Debbas. He had come up the hard way but was driven to make a better life for his family. He went from selling cookies that his mother had baked every day to the soldiers, to owning a dry good store in Beirut. He and my grandmother fell in love and were going to get married. Both of them were young and she was beautiful, and he was a handsome up and coming businessman.

When Saba's mother found out about this love affair and her son being involved with a girl of no family raised in an orphanage, she went and found my grandmother and told her she would kill her if she didn't leave her son alone. She forbid her to love her son and told him the same thing.

My sweet grandmother made the decision on her own to try a move to the USA because she knew she was born in New York. Without telling Saba, she prepared her broken heart and left the orphanage on a boat for Paris. So, alone as a young woman with a broken heart, she left for France. She still had family she had never met in the States and was headed there.

When Saba found out what his mother had done, he became furious with her and went to the orphanage where he was given the information that my grandmother was planning to stay at another affiliated Christian orphanage in Paris while she got her papers in order to venture to the US.

Saba immediately caught a boat to Paris and found her and he married her in Paris! I can't imagine the joy she must have felt, and he never went back as they planned their new life together! They migrated to Havana, Cuba first where he got a job in the hotels, and she went on to New York and joined up with her relatives while she got his paper as her husband to come on Ellis Island. They moved to Duluth, Minnesota with their two boys that she gave him, and there is where my mother was born.

One day when the snow was 10 feet high in Duluth, someone told my grandfather there was a place west of there that had weather like the old country... a place called California! When the snow broke, he bought a model T truck and made the two-month journey to Los Angeles with their furniture, his wife and three children. He eventually became a millionaire in California and raised his family in the stores he owned.

My grandmother was the one person in my life that God used to mold me as the Christian I am today. In Arabic grandmother is called Sitti, so she was Sitti Della. Her love for life and joy in Jesus Christ was so epic it affected everyone she met. She was truly an exceptional lady in every way. I have so many great memories as a kid sitting with her and all of us kids fighting for her attention. She would play games; hold you, scratch our backs, and always give us her full attention. She was an unbelievable master at cooking huge family meals of Arabic food, and we would kill for her rolled grape leaves.

When my father left us and life became real for my family, she would make a trip from downtown LA every Friday with her Pontiac Firebird filled to the brim with groceries and gifts for us, and she would spend the entire day cooking while my mother was at work, and we were at school. Her presence filled our house with joy and every kid we knew would be at our house on Fridays to be around Sitti. It makes me cry as I write this because she was such an example of God's love to all of us ragged kids. Sitti would tell us Bible stories and pray over us and cook huge, delicious meals and then play cards with us or board games late into Friday night. We would laugh all night because she loved to cheat and see if we could catch her!

I remember the street being full of all the neighbor kids as she would leave to go home on Saturday, and she sped away barely looking over the steering wheel in her Firebird. She even let me take the Firebird out and that was an unbelievable thing to do for a kid who wasn't even 16 yet, with no license. When she died of a heart attack at age 69, it rocked our world. There was over 700 people at her funeral! She left a mark on everyone she met! My Sitti left a godly impression on everyone. Fifty years later, I still get asked about her from childhood friends.

As a teenager with anger issues that I felt from my dad deserting us, I rejected God and became an atheist. My unbelief was always countered by the memories of my Sitti, and when God moved on me at 27 years old and freed me from the demons living in me, I gave my life over to Him and realized that my Sitti had prayed for this day many years before. God will use certain people in your life who have made a difference in you that you probably don't realize the impact of their Christian love.

In **Exodus 3:6**, God is telling Moses what He is about to go make Moses do... free the Israelites from slavery in Egypt. Egypt was the most powerful nation on the face of the earth at the time and here is God telling Moses that He is going to send Moses into the Pharaoh and take his slave work force away! Remember that Moses was a part of the Pharaohs house as his mother floated him down the Nile River to save his life: He said also, *"I am the God of your father, the God of Abraham, the God Isaac, and the God of Jacob.*

Then Moses hid his face for he was afraid to look at God."

The point I am trying to make here is that God used Moses hundreds of years later to complete promises that He had made to Abraham, Isaac and Jacob. He used Moses to complete His plan. Do you think it's possible God has made promises to your forefathers? And are those promises playing out in your life today? Do you ever stop your busy life to consider the big picture of your family history and where you fit into God's plan in that lineage?

God used Moses, He worked through Elijah, He used John the Baptist to bring forth Jesus, He used a bunch of wild fishermen, a doctor, and several others. Then He then added Paul to launch the Good News that would change history forever. The past is an enormous spider web of intertwined actions that have been going on for centuries. Your ancestors were survivors, or you wouldn't be here!

The fact is God has blessed every family line alive today in some way and your heritage is part of that. You are a part of something much bigger than yourself, so why is it so hard to realize this and be a proud part of the ongoing mission today? Is God speaking to you today?

Anytime you feel God speaking to you, how you respond depends on how you cultivate your heart. **Luke 8:15** says, *"But the seed in the good soil, these are the ones who have heard the word in an honest and good heart, and hold it fast, and bear fruit with perseverance."*

Are you listening to Him speak to you today with an honest and good heart or are you holding back aligning yourself to the

175

lure of this world and all its tempting satisfactions? The way you respond shows the condition of your heart.

Hosea 10:12 says, *"Sow with a view to righteousness, reap in accordance with kindness; Break up your fallow ground, for it is time to seek the Lord until He comes to rain righteousness on you."* Do we ever stop to question our motives? **Proverbs 16:2** says, *"All the ways of a man are clean in his own sight, but the Lord weighs the motives."* Many things cause us to do the things we do, but it's safe to say the best things we can do are motivated by God with a purpose to see the big picture of how we fit into His plan. The bad things we do come from the wrong motivations like pride, anger, ambition, lust, greed, guilt, fear and hurt from others. It is even possible to do the right things with the wrong motivation. Like going to a Bible study or church with a bad heart or an attitude! An honest and good heart is a humble and thankful one.

Jesus measures our motives by one important standard, Love. Our heart is behind all our actions in this life. Our heart is what is behind the love we show our families, our friends, even the strangers we meet. Oh, yea and don't forget your enemies. Nothing is left to randomness in God's plan for our lives. We tend to think of only the present and what immediate results we are getting, but God has been working for centuries. We get impatient if we can't see the instant results of what He is doing with us. We become aggravated if God intends to finish what He started in us in another person or another generation! Remember, God has been working on your behalf for centuries.

You can start to fix this wrong view by changing your prayer life to one of humbleness and appreciation like Moses did once he stopped fighting God. You can pray for an understanding of the big picture and how God will use you in this grand mystery of history. You can pray for purpose not yet seen. You can pray for courage to put God's plan first above the things of this world. You can pray for a hunger of the living Word of God and start dedicating some of your precious time in this insanely busy world to reading His Word. But most of all, you can pray for an understanding of the big picture and how you fit into your place in Christ... and then pray for the guts to carry it out!

My Sitti watched as her parents were killed, she was deserted by her extended family, and left alone to be raised by Nuns of the Greek Orthodox Church in an orphanage in a 3rd World Country. She was scorned by her mother-in-law, and yet became the greatest Christian woman I have ever met! My Sitti affected everyone she met in a positive way. How does your past compare? This book is part of her legacy! What will your legacy be? Pray for it.

LET'S PRAY...

Jesus, Father God, and the Holy Spirit, thank You for always looking out for me even when I'm stubborn and hard hearted. Thank You for all my ancestors and the many who are in Your presence now, and how You used them and their good and honest hearts to help shape the things of today in my life. Thank You, Lord, for giving me an opportunity to be a blessing to someone in my family and helping me to see people as You see them with love. Help me to be bold and make peace whenever it is up to me.

Help me, Lord, to pray the right prayers that will empower me to carry out Your work for me now, even if You don't finish it in my time. Bind Satan, Lord, and break any and all generational curses against me and my family. Thank You, God, as You move me and use me. Protect my heart and soul, Lord, and help me to always have a smile on my face and a kind word to say. In Jesus' Holy and Mighty name, I pray. **AMEN**

CHAPTER NINETEEN

Prayer and Whiskey Breath

I heard a song one day driving an all-night to Arizona to hunt with my brother Homer Stevens. It was by a band called Love and Theft and it was called, "Whiskey on my Breath." This song spoke to my heart because in my past, I have been in that exact place so many times. That desperate place when all the circumstances of life pile on you and the crushing weight of everything pins you in a chokehold like something you get from a Jujitsu black belt. A seemingly unbreakable chokeholds impossible to defend as the life and breath is being squeezed out of you. The custom in the martial art is to tap out when you know you are beat. Then your opponent will stop the torture and let you go.

In real life, there are many ways to tap out! Some tap out by drinking themselves to death; some tap out by overdosing themselves; some tap out by turning their back on God and surrendering to Satan and his ultimate destruction of their life. Some tap out in very subtle ways like constantly compromising and worming away their lives one day at a time. I believe that our choice to tap out is built inside of every one of us and God will allow our bad choices to get us into chokeholds that only a tap out can save us. Remember, we are creatures of free will! Some of us are so tough and stubborn that we would rather be choked out then tapped out.

One time when my youngest son Cody was a teenager, I grabbed him in a chokehold and started to tell him to tap but he was so tough and strong-willed that he would not tap. I kept the pressure on him until, without really realizing it, I caused him to go unconscious. He went completely limp in my arms, and the second I realized it, I was horrified! It was a game I took too far, and I totally endangered his life.

I laid him down and started doing CPR when he came to with a big smile on his face and drool coming out of his mouth. I can't tell you how happy I was to see light in his eyes again. I told him how sorry I was, and he looked up at me, and said, "I didn't tap!" This was when I realized that this kid had a will of iron that was dangerous to himself! How many of us are the same?

Cody has brought me a million smiles in his young life, as I watched him survive as a rebellious teenager, a mother who caused havoc in our family his entire teen life, and I was shocked when I learned he had joined the Army when he was a junior in high school. He didn't tell anyone until the day he graduated high school and had to get on a bus to Fort Benning, where he would soon become an Infantry man during a time when this country was actively fighting a war. I have never prayed so hard for one of my kids as I did when I watched Cody climb on that bus and drive off to carve out his future path. As anyone who has a kid who has served knows that when they go off to basic, you can't call them, and they can't call you. They are gone and out of touch!

One night about three weeks into his 13-week basic training, Cody called me from Fort Benning crying to tell me he had made a mistake and was going to quit! Cody was going to tap! I was shocked but the way the Army trains them to be soldiers was to completely break them down and make them become part of something way bigger. They become a part of a team taught to fearlessly obey orders even to the point of death. Cody was a hard one to break and he was at the tap out point.

While we were talking, I got a call from my oldest son Tommy. I put Cody on hold, and I said to Tommy, "I got Cody on the other line trying to quit the Army and he is crying and broken." I merged into a three-way call, and Tommy and I began talking some real confidence-building encouragement to motivate Cody into not quitting!

We both pointed out how strong he was, and that Virden's don't quit! The call didn't last too much longer because his drill sergeant was standing next to him listening to his end of the conversation and waiting for his decision to either get him back to the barracks or roll up his stuff and send him home. I led the three of us in a prayer before the phone went dead. I knew the next call

I got would be that he quit and was coming home. But the phone never rang.

Two weeks later, I got a letter from him telling me that he was thankful for the pep talk, and that he was going to make it! I cannot tell you how proud I was of him for sticking it out.

This had happened during a time that I was completely broke and struggling to raise his little sister. But when Family Day and Graduation Day came, I went to one of those quick loan centers and got a title loan on my truck. It was the only asset I had left. I bought a ticket and went to Georgia to be with my son. It was something I would have walked across the country not to miss, and we had the best time together that weekend. He out shot me on the rifle range with M4s, and we got drunk with all his new friends. I met his drill sergeant and he told me Cody was a bad ass and would make a great warrior! Go figure! Go GOD! The kid doesn't know how to tap out.

I spent every dollar I had that weekend, and it was a moment in a dad's life that will never be replaced. I had failed Cody in many ways in his young life but at least I raised a kid with guts and commitment.

The song "Whiskey on my Breath" that I mentioned earlier goes like this: "Oh I know I'm going to Heaven, but I can't go like this, I need to pull myself together before then. Lord, I ain't afraid of dying but what scares me to death, is meeting Jesus with whiskey on my breath."

In life we constantly fall short, and there is a fear that overwhelms us when we fail. Failure causes fear, the ultimate fear is knowing that you contributed to it and your run of bad decisions has backed you into a corner that you can't seem to see daylight from. The essence of this song is that those constant failures strike terror in us, and we start thinking we are going to face our Lord and Master completely out of chances and still screwed up. I believe this fear of the Lord is a proper perspective because the other perspective really gives you less hope!

How do most people think of God? I've heard so many guys refer to God as, "The Big Man Upstairs", "A really cool dude who will let you in if you are just a nice person," "A positive force in a fluffy, white robe and hippie hair sitting back in a big chair holding up the peace sign to all passer byes", or maybe "He is a gentle grandfather figure." The lost people of this world will bring the Creator of the world down to some comfortable level that they can be happy with. But nothing could be further from the truth!

God is to be feared, and not in the way we associate with our parents or other authority figures. He is to be awed in reverence as we are heirs to His kingdom, but He remains and always will our King! The Apostle Paul, in his letter to the Corinthian church, expressed this fact that we must strive to please God either in the body or absent from the body because someday we are going to face Him eye to eye and our lives here will be judged… for the good we've done, or bad!

Knowing that day is coming should motivate us to give it 100%, and not tap! **2 Corinthians 5:8-11**: *"We are of good courage, I say, and prefer rather to be absent from the body and be at home with the Lord.*

Therefore, also we have as our ambition, whether at home or absent, to be pleasing to Him. For we must all appear before the judgement seat of Christ, that each one may be recompensed for his deeds in the body, according to what he has done, whether good or bad. Therefore, knowing the fear of the Lord, we persuade men, but we are made manifest to God, and I hope that we are made manifest also in your consciences."

I don't know about you, but this passage sends chills down my spine! Standing eye to eye with Jesus it will be impossible to hide anything I've said or thought or done in my entire life on earth. Impossible to lie about a thing! Just pure honest evaluation of how I did with the gifts He gave me to work with, the people He put in my care, the children He gave me to raise, the money and productivity He gave me to steward, the countless opportunities He gave me to love my enemies and how I did with all that. Dang, I'm in trouble on the grand scheme of judgement!

I really believe that the way we fear God determines the way we perceive our sin. Otherwise, we wouldn't undertake the Christian life in such a half-hearted way. We excuse sin, worship halfheartedly, go to church (maybe), pray when we can, read the Bible occasionally, be generous to the poor and needy, if it's easy. Most of us are raised like this. It is taught to us that fear is weakness! We are taught this very wrong concept that, "The Big Man Upstairs" needs to be our best friend. Let's not make Christianity too scary!

Our preachers stand at the pulpit and preach, urging us to get saved, repent, get a new best Friend, go to Heaven, He will live inside you and, like a really good dad, protect you from evil. Some of us take it seriously because the Spirit is real and when it happens to you, no one can tell you it didn't! You know something Spiritual outside of your control happened. I explain that to Christians who are scared to death to witness the truth of Jesus because they think, "Oh, I don't know enough Bible verses to share." But that's not the point. The point is telling them about the difference God has made in **your** life! And therein lies the challenge.

It seems that some get the Spirit for a season and then fall back into playing church. They play Christian games and slip down the slippery slope back in the life they had. Then the worry re-enters and the guilt from the sins we run to quickly takes over and we run the marathon with our ankles in shackles terrified that we are going to face Jesus with whiskey on our breath! What does this really mean? What other ways are there than whiskey to indulge our sinful nature in?

I had a cousin who was married and had two beautiful daughters and was crazy rich. He died from a massive heart attack in a hotel room with a hooker and an ounce of cocaine. He was only 50 years old! The truth came out about the way he died, and the family was so grieved for his wife and girls, but I bet when he sits in front of that judgment seat and looks good into the eyes of the Lord, the embarrassment that he caused his family will be the least of his worries! He came to visit me a month before to propose a business deal to my car lot in Bakersfield, and I witnessed to him, but he wanted nothing to do with it! He was a hard-driven businessman and money was his god. I turned down his deal not wanting to be sucked into that lifestyle again because in the past we had made so much money selling drugs together. His funeral was a dark event, and I felt a sad loss over him. Our sin determines the display of our view of God! Our fear of God determines our willingness to tap out to sin and subsequently our work for Him. My cousin died with whiskey on his breath!

In reality, we should be terrified of the power of God! In every case where He appeared to men, they fell on their faces! In **Exodus 20:20,** God sends Moses down Mt. Sinai to warn the people not to come near because to even see Him they would perish! Fearing the Lord should give us confidence to stay away from sin. **Proverbs 16:6** says, *"By lovingkindness and truth inequity is atoned for, and by the fear of the Lord one keeps away from evil."*

Do not let yourself get too comfortable with God! He is the **Creator,** and we are the **created**... Never forget this! We are not His equal in any realm and even though we like to think we are in control of our messy, little world, we are not; He is!

Non-Christians are out there on their own left to sink or swim and the tough ones like to brag about never tapping out. The weak ones fall into a death spiral of addictions and constant victimology excuses that lead to a life of guilt and misery. But we Christians are forgiven, set apart, empowered by one third of the Trinity that lives in us! We are redeemed by the blood of Jesus but know this: **2 Corinthians 5:10,** *"For we must all appear before the judgment seat of Christ, so that each one may be recompensed for his deeds in the body, according to what he has done, whether good or bad."*

Your day of recompense is coming! We should be in absolute

awe of God and fear His wrath enough to get our lives together and conquer our sin patterns because you never know when the lights are going out. You wake up this morning and today is a gift that you will never get back once it's gone... no guarantees that you will be here tomorrow. I urge you to go read **Isaiah 40** and get a proper perspective of God.

There are many ways to die with whiskey on your breath. So how does this affect our prayer life? A proper fear of the Lord will help you change your sin patterns, and that will relieve your guilt. Relieving our guilt will free up our hearts to start taking a meaningful and productive attitude to doing His will in our daily life and that will redirect our prayer life to aligning our prayers to His will for us! Bam!

Philippians 4:5-8 says, *"Let your gentle spirit be known to all men. The Lord is near. Be anxious for nothing, but in everything by prayer and supplication with thanksgiving let your requests be known to God. And the peace of God, which surpasses all comprehension will guard your hearts and your minds in Christ Jesus. Finally, brethren, whatever is true, whatever is honorable, whatever is right, whatever is pure, whatever is lovely, whatever is good repute, if there is anything worthy of praise, let your mind dwell on these things."*

LET'S PRAY...

Dear Father in Heaven, we thank You for the amazing spirit of the Apostle Paul and how You took a mean-spirited hunter and killer of men and turned his life into such a blessing! We ask You for the same measure of grace in our lives. Bring us a joy that comes from aligning our hearts and minds to Your will. Hear our prayers and help us to turn from the traps set by our enemies to make our lives end in a sad and nonproductive way. Give us the courage to face this challenge and the self-worth to strive to be the kind of people You can be proud of. Let us have the sound minds to learn to tap out to the things of this world, the many daily distractions that cripple our ability to serve You with a greater purpose. Help us to not be fearful of facing You eye to eye someday and to be looking forward to You putting Your arms around us and showing us how much You have always loved us. Thank You, Lord, for the chance to serve You because living this life without You is the greatest loss anyone can experience. Help us to be of a thankful heart and share Your love with our messy world! We all miss the mark at times, but in the end Your love and sacrifice for us is enough motivation to never stop trying! Hear my prayer today, Lord and embolden me to do and seek Your will every morning I wake. In the Precious Name of Your Son, Jesus, I lift this prayer to You. **AMEN**

CHAPTER TWENTY

Prayer, Satan and Evil

Almost my entire life I have owned dogs. I got my first dog when I was five years old because I found a stray mutt and brought it home. My dad was mad about this dog, so I hid her out until she became part of the family. Her name was Fluffy. I don't know why I named her that because she wasn't a fluffy dog! Since that time, I have had probably 10 different dogs and, in each case, I have trained these dogs to understand that I was their master.

There are two ways to train a dog. One way is to love the dog, care for it and spend time it, teaching it to obey and rewarding it with love and treats when the dog consistently does what you say. The other way to train a dog is by beating it and intimidating it with fear and pain until it obeys out of fear. Either way will work, but the first way produces a happy dog and one of the rewards of training it by love is every time it sees you come in the door, it will shower your heart with love and excitement.

One of the unique things about dogs is usually they will only consistently obey their own master. I have trained five Labrador Retriever hunting dogs in my life with great success of those dogs only obeying me in the field. If one of my friends would try and make my hunting dogs obey him, it was unlikely that it would obey his commands like it would for me. Occasionally, when training Labradors, you need to show them who is boss.

I have had three males and two females, and the females are much easier to control. The males are hardheaded and need way more correction. So, if you analyze who is the dog going to consistently listen to, it is his master! When the master of the dog gives a command, the dog will perform its task. When someone else gives the dog a command, it considers that person an adversary and decides that it doesn't have to listen. That person then becomes the dog's adversary. Someone giving a command that does not have the authority to command it and it will usually do whatever it wants to do at that point. Why? The one telling it what to do has no authority to command it! Okay, so where am I going with this line of thinking?

As Christian men and women who is our master, and who is our adversary? Simply put, when you give your heart to the Lord, you become an heir to God's kingdom, and He becomes the Master of your life. At that point you submit to His training and learn to obey His commands, and essentially, He becomes the Master of your behavior. He does His training with a level of love for us that is beyond human understanding, and we obey out of love in return. Prayer becomes a method of communication with an unseen Master who is faithful to our best interest at all times, even when we disobey!

On the flip side, Satan is only given authority to command men and women who are not children of God, and who has no real authority over the Christian people of the world. But here is the part that a lot of Christians don't understand. We don't have authority over Satan in this world! So, if we don't, then who does? Who is Satan's master? The answer is simple. Only God, our Master is Master over Satan! Satan has no obligation to listen to us anymore than my hunting dog has any inclination to retrieve a down bird for one of my friends trying to get my dog to obey! In this life, Satan is our adversary!

In **1 Peter 5:8**, the Bible says, *"Be of sober mind, be on the alert. Your adversary, the devil, prowls about like a roaring lion, seeking for someone to devour."* Clearly Satan is our adversary in the Christian life! In **Ephesians 6:12,** the Apostle Paul explains to us in his introduction of the full armor of God, *"For our struggle is not against flesh and blood, but against the rulers, against the powers, against the world forces of this darkness, against the spiritual forces of wickedness in heavenly places."* Where are the heavenly places?

We sometimes have this vision of heavenly places being free of evil. Satan and all his evil angels came from Heaven. They were created by God and, at one time, Satan was God's crowning angel. The Bible says that Satan sinned against God by wanting to become like God, and God set him apart from His heavenly place with all the angels Satan had perverted. Those who have become his workforce here with one purpose... to destroy the souls of God's Creation—us!

However, if you look closely at the story of Job, Satan is in Heaven talking to God, and God asks him what he has been up too. Obviously, God, who know everything already, knew his answer and when Satan tells Him that he has been roaming Earth looking for someone to destroy, God offers up Job. Clearly Satan has access to heavenly places and can do his evil work because God has given him authority of this world that is not directly in line with God.

Poor Job! Why would God volunteer him for the horrific shake down he was about to get? Even Satan argues with God saying that Job is under His protection and all Job's success is because God has blessed him and protected him for being an extremely faithful man. God gives Satan permission to take from him anything he wants, but limits him from taking Job's life. God is about to prove that this man will not turn his back on God... no matter what Satan does to him!

So, Satan, in one fell swoop, destroys, and kills everything Job has, including all his wealth (and by today's standards, Job was a billionaire), he kills his children, and when the news starts to come into Job, he is beyond destroyed emotionally, but refuses to curse God.

Then Satan returns and gets permission to infect him with sickness and even then, Job doesn't break and curse God! God would not allow Satan to kill Job. Who has authority over Satan?

Only God. We don't have authority over Satan, God does. We are not Satan's master just because we are Christians. The devil does not have to answer to us no matter how loud we yell. I shudder when I hear people taking on Satan and his demons in their own authority! They have no clue what they are up against! I know this from a very personal level because the night I gave my life to Christ I was demon possessed.

I was selling cocaine for about seven years and was controlling a huge business moving about eight kilos of cocaine a week. The problem was, I was using about an ounce of pure cocaine a week for my personal habit and was getting ever closer to death or prison at any moment. I was driven by an evil force inside me that I had no control or understanding of, and my actions had an evil ripple effect into the lives of many people.

The drugs I was selling and the power I wielded had destroyed many men and women and I didn't care. I was addicted to many things and had an unsatiable appetite for women and would use the drugs to trade for sex, even though I was married and had a baby boy. Very few people messed with me because I had connections to men who would cross any line to do my dirty work because I could pay them anything they asked for. I had evil alliances on a 360-degree compass all around me and little by little it was always pushing the envelope of disaster.

One night when I had had a bad experience with my wife as she complained that I had never even held my baby boy, something flipped in my spirit, and I started to question all of my terrible ways. I did not get high that night on Thai stick weed which was opiated weed that I used to come down and sleep.

I was awake and restless and decided to get up and go sneak in some porn. My wife and baby son Tommy were asleep. I went to the den and turned the tv on, turned the volume down and laid on the couch in my $1000 robe and began flipping channels with no lights on in the house looking for the once-a-week soft porn movie the cable channels played in those days. I couldn't find it and wound-up on the Christian Satellite Network listening to a street preacher named Mario Murillo lashing out at cocaine dealers!

I started to laugh and thought that, hey, is he talking to me? And he was. That night as I bent my knees to Christ, a demon so dark and powerful came out of my body and to this day has scared me straight. I talk about it in the story "Crossroads Untaken" that I mentioned a few chapters back. But for now, I am going to tell you that I was indeed demon possessed, and I was freed from that cocaine demon that night and my entire life changed.

God had rescued me from certain early death or decades in prison when I was trying to watch porn! Instantly I had a new Master! Satan was no longer my master after that night, and ever since, I have been moving my heart and life toward my new Master, Jesus Christ.

The point is that demon did not answer to me! Only God is Satan's Master, and all his demons are subject to the power of God! Understanding this epic concept is so important to how you view you place in the order of things and will affect your prayer life and your ability to find protection from evil only under the heavenly wings of God's protection. **James 4:7** says, *"Submit therefore to God. Resist the devil and he will flee from you."* By submitting to God's will in our life, God will give us the power to resist the devil, and by God's authority, not our will, the devil will flee from us. Submit! Resist!

We must be connected to Satan's Master, God, if we want to out power, outsmart and win against the evil forces of darkness set against us here. We must have His help because we don't have the authority over evil on our own! Satan's main goal is to poison our hearts and take our eyes off God, and His will for us, and put it back on the tempting things of this world. What happens to us when we cave into this scheme? We lose faith and start to question and compromise!

I have counseled many young women who think they are running out of time to get married and will compromise the one thing they shouldn't and get involved with an unbeliever, because they're desperate and have lost faith in God's ability to bring them the one that He has planned for them. It always ends bad! But they do it over and over with the same results. It starts a vicious cycle, and it goes like this; the enemy's goal is to get our eyes off Christ and back on the things of this world that we falsely think we can control. When our focus is on anything but Christ, we lose heart, and when we lose heart, we lose faith, and when we lose faith, we lose prayer, and when we lose prayer, we are like a lost satellite wondering around space with no communications waiting for gravity to take over and crash us down to destruction. And guess what? Satan has victory, and another life that had purpose for

God is destroyed, and another testimony diminished!

The opposite is true as well. You keep your faith alive and thriving by staying focused on Jesus Christ through prayer. If you are lacking faith, undoubtedly you will be lacking in prayer which will in turn cause a deeper lack of faith! They go together like gasoline and a match... prayer is the match, and faith is the fire that it ignites!

Can you evoke your prayers to Satan's Master to defeat his schemes in your life divinely? No, not on your own, but through the unlimited power of Jesus Christ. The power of Jesus Christ through the Holy Spirit will make his schemes vanish. Jesus is the inventor and author of faith! **Hebrews 12:2** say, *"Fixing our eyes on Jesus, the author and perfector of faith, who for the joy set before Him endured the cross, despising the shame and has sat down at the right hand of the throne of God."*

If we could jump into a time machine and be dropped off in Palestine in the days Jesus was working all His miracles and doing His ministry, we would be so motivated to never lose our faith and ability through prayer to communicate to Him. Imagine watching Him pull enough food out of a small basket to feed 5000 people and have leftovers as they sat out in the country on a hill! The people were so hungry for His words that they sat there all day not worrying about what they were going to eat that night. Jesus, knowing this, fed them. The disciples were blown away.

Then Jesus decides to get away and jumps in a boat with His experienced crew of fishermen and decides to cross the water to the other side where His Word has not gone out. Along the way they hit a bad storm at sea and are in such trouble that these hardened seamen are about to sink, and where is Jesus? Sleeping like a baby in the bottom of the boat! In desperation they wake Him. I used to fish the open sea when I was younger, and nothing will send terror through your heart like a storm at sea when you can't see land! What does Jesus do? He wakes up and laughs at them, and with a Word stops the storm and calms the sea! They are blown away.

They get where they are going and an extremely demon-possessed man who has been chained over and over again, because he is such a threat to the local population, runs up to Jesus. That alone probably scared and freaked out the disciples... and what occurs? The demons, not the man, instantly recognize Jesus, and they beg for mercy not to be sent to the abyss but be allowed to enter a herd of pigs grazing on the hillside cliffs above the sea. For some reason, Jesus agrees to cut the demons some slack and they leave the tortured man at His command and a legion of demons go into the pigs possessing them instead. And the entire herd of pigs commit suicide by running off the cliff into the sea and drown! The freed man begs Jesus to be allowed to follow him and Jesus says no and sends him back into his village to tell the world about the great things He has done. Free of Satan and his demons, Jesus puts this man to work!

We are no different. Once we get saved, we want to hide out in church and be around our safe little Christian world, and hypothetically follow Jesus around protected by being in His bubble. That is not the game! Jesus wants you to get out and tell of His saving grace! Free of Satan and his demons, your testimony is powerful and will change the lives of the people around you. Your faith will grow as you obey and see the power you wield in the name of Christ. As your faith grows your prayers will become powerful, your heart will go fearless to the dark side, and you will be openly praying for all people and all power to beat back the evil forces set against us in this life.

When was the last time you prayed with a desperate stranger? You know, when the Holy Spirit is telling you to, but it's just too embarrassing to break out in faith and ask, "Can I pray for you right now, this moment?" Or do you really think He wants you hiding behind His hippie robe and peace sign attitude waiting for Him to act so you can cheer Him on? It is sad to see the American church being so distracted by the things of the world, the consumerism of the Word that in essence nothing meaningful is happening in a country where so many are falling off the cliff and drowning.

The homeless multiple daily, the elderly pile up in pathetic care corrals, the youth are committing suicide at never-before rates. Marriages and homes across this country are decaying, the crime and violence is becoming uncontrollable, and **where is the church in all this?** Hiding in their multi-million dollar buildings and waiting for Him to return!

If you want to defeat the power of Satan first in your prayer life, you must understand that you do not have the tools to do that. You do not have authority over Satan and his army of evil disruptors. But with Christ in your heart and Christ on your tongue, your prayers will command a power that will make them run!

God has given me a gift of recognizing demons as I meet people and when I cross one of them, we instantly clash. One night when my group was feeding the homeless, a woman sitting alone way in the back with her back turned to me, homeless, dirty and probably starving, jumped five feet in the air when I tried to fill her Styrofoam cup with milk. She spun around and our eyes met, and she lashed out at me in fear. Screaming "Leave me alone!" As she jumped out of the chair, the table overturned and she grabbed her backpack and ran out of the dining room screaming, "Get away from me!" It scared me half to death and I instantly knew that demon inside her saw Christ in me and drove that poor woman back out into the freezing, snowy night in Reno. Hungry and desperate, she ran! The commotion stopped the entire serving to the hundred other homeless being served by my community group. I didn't chase after her, and instead decided to let her run and get on with feeding people and pouring milk and sharing the love of Christ in real time.

Is that what Jesus wants is for us to be out among the lost fighting the forces of evil or complaining when Sunday comes around and we force ourselves to spend an hour and a half hiding behind our preachers and sermons? I am not saying church is not great and getting the Word by professional preachers is not important, but we must remember that we are all called in different ways to do His work! So, look into your heart and be honest. Ask yourself first, then turn to Him in prayer and figure out how to use His power to beat back the subtle evil influences Satan is using to lessen your ability to get out there in the fight! Soldier up! It's time.

Look at **Philippians 4:6-7** again, *"Be anxious for nothing, but in everything by prayer and supplication with thanksgiving let your requests be made known to God and the peace of God which surpasses all comprehension, shall guard your hearts and minds in Christ Jesus."* Guard your hearts and minds from what? SATAN!

LET'S PRAY...

Father God, we are powerless over Satan and evil. We know and understand without Your protection we have no authority over the forces of evil. So we ask in the most serious and sincere way that You protect us from evil, that You give us the kind of hearts and purpose to face the dark side with a complete confidence that comes from being one of Your powerful children. We ask for courage to get back out into the battles of this life empowered by the Holy Spirit to do Your work and affect the lives of our lost friends and relatives. We ask for the boldness to pray with hurting strangers on the streets of our towns. We ask for the guts to speak out at our jobs and for the power to live Godly lives and not bring shame to Your causes. Give us this amazing work to do, Lord. Help us to seek peace with everyone and to be instruments of love, not hate and bitterness. Change our hearts to be peacemakers and forgive the ones who hurt us and to love our current enemies! We know Satan is real and he commands the evil forces at work here, but we seek to be used by You, Lord, to counter his evil plans and move our brothers and sisters to a safe camp at Your feet! Help us to be real warriors, not tasteless salt hiding in Your churches and just waiting for You to fix it all. In the name of Jesus Christ our Lord. **AMEN**

CHAPTER TWENTY-ONE

Prayer and Peace

The entire world wants peace but cannot seem to ever find it. Peace in Middle East? Arabs and Jews hate each other. Peace in Afghanistan and a 20-year war that just ended badly. Peace in the Orient where China is always threatening, North Korea launching missiles, Iran cooking up uranium and making nuclear bombs.

Then just look right here at home! Racial violence for the last year, riots, no one is at peace, crime in all the major cities rising at incredible rates and people are scared. Webster defines peace as, "a freedom from struggle, a freedom from disturbance, quiet and tranquility, a freedom from war, calm." All this world tension and violence just adds to our already complicated lives!

When you think about struggles, we add to all this in our own minds with worrying and stressing about our families, our relationships, our jobs and careers, our education and future, and our acceptance into a circle of friends who won't judge us for our faults. It's no wonder we have a mental health problem; people are quitting and living on the streets or going crazy and shooting up everything and everyone!

I don't know why God set all this into motion after the sin of Adam and Eve, but from that moment on peace has been a pipe dream in this world. Babies are born struggling from the gate and raising them is no picnic either! Our children give us a million smiles and special moments along life's journey, but they are also the reason our hair falls out or turns grey too quickly.

It is a fact that we are born with this sin nature, and we are taught along the way to do what? Fight back! Every time we confront an unpeaceful situation, we naturally fight back because we want control. When we try and take control, we create confrontation. The natural cycle in confrontation is more conflict and the elusive state of peace never seems to happen. Plus, there are always negative consequences in conflict and people get hurt. In wars, people get killed; in civil violence, cities and businesses get destroyed; in family arguments, feelings get hurt when terrible things are said!

In any event, conflict begets hurt either physically or emotionally. We are trained to get through it and try to heal ourselves, but the scars change us from the inside out. Divorce, which is one of the most damaging life events, seems to harden us and make us so weary of future relationships. Children of divorce sit back and suffer, and they vow to never be like their parents.

They decide that a piece of paper means nothing and elect to live together instead. All this conflict going on around us seems unbeatable!

I have deep empathy for non-Christians in this regard because they are left to tread boiling water with a 600-foot tidal wave looming in the distance that they can see and know eventually that, no matter what they do, it's still coming!

On the other hand, as Christians, we have hope! We have the ability to pray, and a confidence that no matter the situations we face, God is on our side. We will know peace in the middle of the worst times, and eventually we will know a peace that we have never experienced before on Earth when we are transformed and in the presence of Jesus in Heaven.

Think back in your life to that one special Christian person who always had a smile on their face and a positive word on their lips. They always seemed at peace with a certain step and keen eye to looking at the conflict in life through the lens of Christ. That person knew just how to pray and trust the promises of God!

How many of us have been at death's door at the hands of others and never lost our cool because we knew that God was in control? Like Stephen, the first martyr who was stoned to death and never fought back. Then there was Peter who was sentenced to death and chained in a Roman jail cell singing hymns to God throughout the night, and God caused an earthquake and sent angels to free him. Then Paul, when he was shipwrecked as a prisoner on his way to be tried in Rome facing certain death, he didn't try and escape. He helped save who he could and faced the future with confidence and love toward his guards. What kept them all in the game? What common denominator did they all have that we struggle to find today? It was prayer and trust that God had them in His hand.

Here is a hard cold fact; this world we live in will never be at peace and we will have problems as long as we live in this dispensation. We are called to be different and see things from a different perspective because we are set apart and given a special purpose here on earth.

The first thing we need to do is stop trying to fix and control the unrest around us. We need to learn to pray for wisdom on how to act and be an instrument of God's plan. God is merciful and desires that no soul should perish, so He waits to clean this mess up until all of us do the best job we can sharing the hope and peace with the lost world. You don't have to look too hard around you to find a hurting person! They are everywhere! But we get so hung up in our own misery that we blind ourselves to the hurting world around us.

The world loves to point a hard finger at us Christians and they are quick to point out what hypocrites we are! Why? Because most of the time we deserve it! We talk the things of the next world, but we do not demonstrate it well in our daily walk.

So, if you want to know how to find peace in your hearts as you, too, tread in this whirlpool of unrest, the first thing you need to do is realize your place in the grand scheme of things. Then for the sake of the others around you, start acting like Stephen as the rocks flew at hit his flesh, he prayed for all of his killers!

The brave and solid way he died made such an impression on Saul who stood by and held the coats of the men killing Stephen that eventually Saul became the Apostle Paul. Are there Saul's out there in your world that you can help shape up for Kingdom work?.

Isaiah 26:3-4 says, *"You keep him in perfect peace whose mind is stayed on you because he trusts you. Trust in the Lord forever, for the Lord God is an everlasting Rock."* What does that mean *"whose mind is stayed on you"*? It means that there is a type of person whose faith is so strong that no matter what flaming arrows are coming at them, they keep their thoughts on God. Does it mean they aren't scared? Heck no! It means that they have a keen sniper-type focus on God and the bigger picture God wants us to see, and that focus creates a trust in Him to work out all things for our good.

Are we that type of Christians? We have choices to make at every turn in life. We can stop and feel sorry for ourselves. We can quit and start a litany of excuses at how hard the world is to navigate. We can blame everyone and everything else around us and focus on how unfair and difficult life is. Or we can take the high road and climb into a steadfast mindset of trust in His ways and find peace in the middle of the rocks flying at our heads!

Romans 12:17-21 says, *"Never pay back evil for evil to anyone. Respect what is right in the sight of all men. If possible, so far as it depends on you, be at peace with all men. Never take your own revenge, beloved, but leave room for the wrath of God, for it is written 'vengeance is mine, I will repay,' says the Lord. To the contrary, if your enemy is hungry feed him, if he is thirsty give him something to drink, for by* *doing so you will pour burning coals on his head. Do not be overcome by evil but overcome evil with good."* The key in this passage for us to see here is the statement, *"as far as it depends on you."* That means we are to be quick minded enough not to lose our cool in tough situations and look for ways to be a peacemaker, not an escalator of conflict. Granted there might be situations that are out of our control, and we may need to defend those we love or even the innocent, but they will be rare.

Most of the peace that eludes our daily life can be mitigated with instant prayer and loving display of the power of God in our minds and hearts! The craziness of this world isn't going to fix itself, and God has a grand plan to clean it all up in the future. The important thing for us to realize is how we can be instruments of peace on a minute-by-minute basis. Learn to trust God through your quick-draw prayers in all situations. *"As far as it depends on you."* Forgive!

Forgiveness is not always easy. In fact, at times forgiveness feels more painful than the wound we suffered. But there is no peace without forgiveness. After all, Christ forgave us and continues to forgive us our sins on an ongoing basis! Mother Teresa once said, "Peace begins with a smile." Let's try that!

LET'S PRAY...

Dear Father of Peace, help us to have a mindset of peace. Help us to keep our focus on the mission field around us that we can affect by showing grace and peace to everyone around us. Help us forgive with pure hearts and mend relationships with friends and family. Help us to be neutral to the conflicts in this world and in our country so that we may be instruments of peace and not fan the flame of hate that Satan is stoking now in our world. Please, God, give us confidence that no matter what rocks are flying our way, the pain of the blows will be nothing compared to the glory we will see someday when we sit at your feet and know true eternal peace. When the lion and the lamb will sit next to each other, and no fear will be present. Help us to be solid in our purpose and realize that true peace lies within our hearts and not in the world around us. In Christ Holy name, I pray. **AMEN**

CHAPTER TWENTY-TWO

Effective Prayer

Why do some prayers seem to work, and others never do? What causes this to be such a mystery? Why can't God just be cool and answer all of our prayers the way **we** want? I believe there are three main reasons for this and before we find out that our prayers are effective, we must grasp onto these three facts concerning prayer:

1. The way we pray.

2. What we pray for.

3. Our faith as we pray, or the lack there of.

We need to have a clear understanding that God created us with the ability to know that we matter. In my past criminal life and when I was an atheist, I used to say that ultimately nothing mattered. That gave me the ability to move around this evil world that I was part of and do the evil things I was doing without a conscience. It was a convenient way to check out of any long-term responsibility for my decisions and consequences. An "ultimately nothing matters" attitude is an amazing way to justify anything, and when you surround yourself with others who believe the same, the terrible decisions you make seem to be an easy choice.

In that mind frame, all you care about is the moment! How much money can I make from stealing whatever thing I'm seeking? How much pleasure can I get from taking advantage of some girl? How much of a rush can I feel by out running the police? What kind of power will I wield when I beat this rival gang at their own game and take their territory? So, my statement is true; "God created us with the ability to matter, even if we live on the dark side of life and are using our ability to matter in selfish and evil ways!"

All our decisions have enormous consequences! Once you understand this then the ability to start measuring the things you are doing to the results that they are having in your life and to those around you, begin to have clarity which is extremely scary. For non-believers and people engulfed in the pursuit of the world, the drive to achieve something always pushes them to do what is best for them. It is basic human nature to do what is best for you and at all costs.

How many marriages have been destroyed when one of the spouses decides that this marriage is not in their best interest anymore, even though the other spouse begs for solutions and becomes the heartbroken person who is left behind? The one who is causing the hurt walks away in their sin knowing what they are doing is wrong, yet are still compelled to continue despite the fact that they know it's wrong. So, they go to their own twisted kind of prayer claiming, "their right to choose and be happy".

The problem is that they are never happy, and their hearts harden over time. They justify constantly to themselves that the consequences of their decisions were bad luck! The one left behind may turn in self-pity and anger and, at first, beg God for a miracle. Then when that doesn't work out for them, they begin to boil inside with resentment and hate and, in doing so, poison themselves and their prayer life.

In **1 Kings 18**, we get to witness what an effective prayer looks like. The profit Elijah demonstrates his prayer and the result of his faith. The land was in a terrible 3-year drought that Elijah had prayed for; all the crops were dried up, all the livestock was dead. There was no water to be found and life was ceasing to exist. The food sources for the people were disappearing and they were starving. God tells Elijah to go up on a mountain with his servant and pray for rain. Elijah goes up and crouches with his head in his knees and starts to pray. He prays for a while and doesn't even look for a cloud. Then he sends his servant to go look at the sky. They could see the sea from where they were, but there wasn't a cloud in the sky.

Elijah starts to pray again. The story doesn't say how long he prayed between each time, but it does say Elijah never looked up. He sent his servant each time and there was no cloud. Elijah, with his head down and his purpose aligned with God's will, prayed with a determination! He prayed in total faith that God was going to bring water and life back to the land. This went on six times, and every time he prayed, the servant reported no clouds.

Elijah kept praying and on the seventh time, his servant reported to him that there was the tiniest cloud as far as you could see... so small your finger could cover it in the distance. Elijah looked up and told the servant to get off the mountain and go tell the King that rain was coming, and not just a little but a down pour! So much so, in fact, that if he didn't get off the mountain right then, he wouldn't make it.

The servant probably thought Elijah was crazy. A tiny cloud a million miles away is going to cause a flood? It never says how long the prophet prayed, but he prayed and sent his guy seven times to check for clouds. I imagine this wasn't a quick prayer, yet his faith not to stop praying is an example for us, and the result was an incredible storm that brought an end to the devastating drought.

Why do you think God used Elijah? Do you think you are any different than Elijah? If so, in what ways are we different? He was a man just like us. He was trying to do God's will in his life, just like most of us. What separates us is the faith in which Elijah prayed and the way we pray. I venture by comparison, our prayers are Casper milk toast prayers compared to Elijah's.

Augustine said once, "Without God we cannot and without us God will not." God wants us active and alive and looking for ways to show His greatness and willingness to answer our prayers to the lost people here. That is exactly what Elijah was doing. Elijah didn't run down the mountain and say, "Hey, let's throw a party for me! I caused the rain to come and it ended a terrible drought." He ran down and gave the glory to God!

In our world, the decisions of men and angel's matter. Can we really change things with our prayers? Elijah was bound and determined to see things change at the hand of God. Are we, or do we take a stab at it and give up after a while? When would you have quit? The second time? The third time?

Elijah was sitting on rocks crouched down with his head between his knees. How long before you start to get cramped up? The fourth or fifth time? What could he be praying different between each time? Do we let the evidence of no answer discourage us from continuing not to pray? Elijah did not let the evidence discourage him, and however long it took, he was going to stay in the game!

Are we that determined when we pray? Do we give up because nothing is happening? Let's look at **James 5:16-20**, *"Therefore, confess your sins to one another, and pray for one another, so that you may be healed. The effective prayer of a righteous man can accomplish much. Elijah was a man with a nature like ours, and he prayed earnestly that it would not rain, and it did not rain on the earth for three years and six months. Then he prayed again, and the sky poured rain and the earth produced its fruit. My brethren, if any among you strays from the truth, and someone turns him back, let him know that he who turns a sinner from the error of his ways will save his soul from death, and will cover a multitude of sins."* The Apostle James is making a killer point here, that we are just like Elijah, mortal men and women, and our prayers can make a difference if we are righteous, and we pray with a determination that is modeled like Elijah! In other words, we can do it!

So, search your hearts and obey the word. If there are sin patterns in your life, find a strong brother and or sister in the Lord and confess your sin **(1 John 1:9)** and begin a good work inside you to fix those problems. Then start an effective prayer life... one prayer at a time. Seek out the purpose God has for you in this life and look for hurting people to pray with. Be the one in your crowd they come to when they are hurting and in need of prayer. We are just like Elijah, but how are we praying effectively, with faith, like Elijah or are we praying Casper milk toast prayers?

LET'S PRAY...

Dear Lord in Heaven above and Master of all things created by You, hear our prayers today. Help us to be a righteous example of what You want us to be in the world You have spun around us. Help us and give us the solid faith to pray like Elijah with a determination in our prayers that will prompt You to grant our prayers because we pray for things You want us to do, and not for ridiculous things of this world. Thank You, Lord, for giving us a chance to serve You and to be a part of Your eternal plan in this crazy world we live in. Give us a desire so strong that the love of Jesus never leaves our smile. Fix our hearts on You, Lord because we know and understand You look at the heart. We love You, Father. In Jesus' Righteous Name we pray. **AMEN**

CHAPTER TWENTY-THREE

Pray Like a Real Man or Woman

The book you are reading came from a series of Bible studies with car salesmen, businessmen and a few church guys, too. It was a study that I did at my house, led by God on each lesson to mostly unchurched men in order to share the Word with them. It was comical at times and probably could have gone viral if recorded because the stories they shared, the foul language they used, and the characters sitting in my den did match what most Christians would consider a Bible study. The struggle for them to find verses as we studied added much time, but it was a blessing to see them with a Bible in their lap looking for Zacharias or a little book like 1st John.

I would watch as the church guys eagerly help the rest find the chapter and verse, and then asked them to read it aloud. For some, it was the first time they had ever read any Bible verse aloud. The power of the Holy Spirit was strong in that room, and we always ended praying for each other's needs, which brought real tough men to tears as God softened them to each other and to the things of the Spirit. This lesson was aimed at the macho egos we all have and how real men act both in the world and in the Christian world, despite that it was aimed at modern men. I believe the lesson is an important one even for women, so I included it in this book.

When we think of real men in this time in history, we think of the images the advertising world has drilled into our heads, like the Marlboro Man, a tough cowboy image. A man who is strong, brave, and who will fight anyone, anytime. A man who has courage and honor, and money and success, who owns a lot of stuff and drives big trucks or fast cars, and has a good woman who never talks back. He also has great kids who are all going off to colleges with full-ride scholarships. He controls his world and really doesn't need to pray because he can handle his life. Why does the world hold all men to that standard? Because it sells and we eat it up!

The two main problems with this are that we are all human and we all are not that guy. We may try to be, but sooner or later we will find ourselves in the foxhole with the surprises of life bullets zinging over our heads. The second reason is we have been conditioned as men to handle our own problems! Man up, we are told!

The Christian man by contrast is seen as a weak, venerable,

grateful servant. He lives by a code of love and honesty. He looks for ways to help the weak instead of storm on them and use them to further his position or wealth. He takes the beating and turns the other cheek and puts his faith in eternal treasure, not the things of this world.

The Christian man's code is completely different. God-like lifestyle verses the prevailing culture. It all breaks down to what your life is anchored in. That is, what defines you as a man or a woman. You can see it in the Apostle John where he says in **John 3:30**, *"He must increase, but I must decrease."* Speaking of Jesus in His life and having a servant's heart, weaned of being arrogant but it's so hard not to be when you have been trained that way.

Or, if you're not the arrogant type, maybe you're the quiet type. The one who tries to believe, but when things don't go your way, you get angry and resentful and rebellious, and you turn your back on God and His plan for your life. You go on and make your own plans, but we are warned about this, too!

James 4:13-17, *"Come on now you who say, 'Today or tomorrow we shall go to such and such a city and spend a year there and engage in business and make a profit.' Yet you do not know what your life will be tomorrow. You are just a vapor that appears for a little while and then vanishes away. Instead, you ought to say, 'If the Lord wills, we should live and also do this or that.' But as it is, you boast in your arrogance; all such boasting is evil. Therefore, to one who knows the right thing to do, and does not do it, to him it is sin."* And we know that this type of sin based in our attitude directly affects how God responds to our prayers.

We will never get it all right, but if we are moving in the right direction, we are making progress and God sees the heart. He knows our weakness, but He loves it when we replace the cocky world attitude with a servant's heart!

The hardest part of this paradigm shift is to realize as Christians that we are all called to a greater purpose in this life, even if we do not immediately see it. In the book of **James 1:13** is one of the greatest chapters in the Bible about understanding our purpose, despite the circumstances we suffer in here.

James explains that God cannot be tempted by evil, and He will never tempt us. Instead, we are carried away by our own lusts and that the wrong doings we fall into greatly affect our attitude and our behaviors. We are given free and constant access to God, and we can ask for wisdom anytime, and He will give it to us as long as we ask with a humble heart, and we do not doubt that He will answer us.

The temporal things of this world fade away and, in the end, we are left with the sum of all the decisions we made in our lives toward God. Just go to any funeral service or celebration of life and see what is said about that person. How did they leave the ones around them? Better off with a life that, despite the hardships, always pointed to faith or is it a sad testimony to what they had or built in this world that is now being left behind for the vultures to pick through? Having a heart that is soft for the hurting people around you and one that is not embarrassed to talk about the things of God that create hope in those as only a relationship with Jesus can do, I dare to say is a legacy for real men, and for real women too!

In **James 1:17** it says, *"Every good thing given and every perfect gift is from above, coming down from the father of lights, with whom there is no variation or shifting shadow."* The men and women of this world do not get this concept. They struggle to find joy and happiness in the things of this world which always disappoint, and in the end of life when the vapor turns to mist and our souls are leaving our frail bodies, a sinking sorrowful regret overcomes them, because they realize how much they missed not being aligned to the Creator of their life and what great things He had planned for them,

So, let's be joyful in the trials of the life of real men and women and let's give thanks that He allows us to learn from our mistakes as we grow in wisdom and grace. Let us forgive those who hurt us for the greater good of showing them a glimpse of grace through faith in the things to come!

LET'S PRAY...

Dear Mighty Father of Lights, help us to not fall into a life built on the lies and false promises of the Marlboro man, and instead, give us eyes to see the future with You in eternity with all of the people we love there with us, because they saw a glimpse of Your greatness and peace in us while we were here, and they had a chance to share You. Make our lives count for something eternal! Change our life goals to not be ones that fall short of Your mission for us here on Earth. Protect our hearts from Satan and his lies to always turn us from the pure things of this world You give us to the things here that are so inadequate in fulfilling our life with eternal happiness. Thank you, Lord, for the opportunity to understand this great calling You give us and to always be moving in the right direction despite the mistakes we make. Thank You for Your patience and grace for us that never ends! Help us to always acknowledge You in all circumstances, especially the tough times as we develop into sharp tools You can use in the lives of those around us. I lift these prayers to You, Father, in Jesus' name. **AMEN**

CHAPTER TWENTY-FOUR

How To Have Effective Prayer?

There are three main reasons why some prayers work, and some prayers don't... The way we pray, what we pray for, and our faith or lack of it!

When we go back and look at Elijah, we see that God told him to pray for a drought and the world dried up for three and a half years. Desperate times upon the people, when we think of a drought today, we think, "Oh no, I can only water my grass every other day or I need to take quicker showers." But the story in **1 Kings** is much more serious. The crops were completely gone, the livestock was dead or dying off, the people were dying off, and I'm sure the weak ones like the older and younger ones were suffering the most. No food, no water, and when God askes Elijah to go pray for rain we see a savage response to prayer from him.

Elijah knows that he has no option but to do what God said, until it happens! It's life and death for everyone! He goes up the mountain and begins to pray, and over and over he fails, but his servant keeps reporting no change! Again, he goes at it, probably sitting or kneeling on rocks uncomfortably, probably no water bottles laying around, probably hot as heck up there, and he keeps praying and praying! Is this the way we pray? Do we pray with this kind of commitment? I doubt seriously that many of us do.

We want something from God; we want a change in our lives, we want someone else's life changed, we want to sit for a minute and conjure up God, and then ask Him for a quick favor so we can get back to our busy life. We really don't believe in our heart of hearts that He is going to respond, and getting our way from Him is probably harder that winning the lottery, but, hey, let's give it a shot. Kind of like buying a scratcher ticket. Maybe we will get lucky... maybe we won't! How different do we approach prayer than Elijah in these three key areas?

Are we going all in with our prayer discipline or merely scratching the ticket with a penny we found in our drink holder as we speed off to another more important obligation in our day?

As Augustine said, "Without God we cannot, and without us, He will not."

James 5:16 says, "Therefore, confess your sins to one another, and pray for one another, so that you may be healed. THE EFFECTIVE PRAYER OF A RIGHTEOUS MAN CAN ACCOMPLISH MUCH." I capitalized the last part of this verse so it will sink in. Are you or do you have a trustworthy friend or family member that you can open up to and confess your sins to? Who do you pray for and listen to their confessions with? When was the last time you sat with a friend or loved one who is faithful and you bared your soul? Is it possible to be healed without doing this? Why do you think God had the Apostle James tell us this?

There are two main parts to this that we must understand. First, effective prayer and second, a righteous man. If you are feeling left out from God answering your prayers, then you are probably thinking one of three things. His promises are not true, the Scripture is not real, or is nothing happening for a reason?

First, let's look at what it means to be a righteous man. Does that mean we don't sin? No! God looks past our sin through the window of Jesus. He looks to our hearts... beyond our thoughts and actions to the condition of our hearts. If our prayers aren't working, we need to look inward at our hearts!

Do we confess before we pray? **1 John 1:9** assures us that He will forgive us when we ask from the heart. You confess, He forgives! You should clear the slate before you come before the Almighty God of the universe. Or are our hearts confused and concerned with the problems of this world, such as money, goals, work, addictions, or any other distractions that Satan can cloud up our hearts with?

Whose mission are we on? Is it our own mission for our life or is it His mission for our life? Are we actively helping others in this area by praying with them and sharing our faith, or do we just want to take all the time? It's the old adage of having a catcher's mitt on both hands... It's hard to play catch this way!

The other side of this equation is, do we pray fervently? Do we quit easily? Do we pray for the day when we wake up and say, "Good Morning" to our Lord? Are we praying during the busy lives we have for every little turn that can harden our hearts? Do we pray in public, in restaurants giving thanks before we eat? Seems like an embarrassing moment that we would rather not do, but how does God look at that decision?

You have a chance to open a discussion with eternal consequences with others who could need prayer and instead, elect not to embarrass yourselves. Do we pray at night as we shut off the lights on another day and rethink the events of that day, analyzing what we might have done better? Do we ask forgiveness before we go lights-out or are we going into our sleep time angry with someone or some situation?

Morning, noon, and night are we keeping our mind in check and practicing a prayer discipline that truly comes from a grateful heart? Are we living our lives putting the greatest command in front of all we do? **1 Peter 4:7-8** says, *"The end of all things is at hand, therefore be of sound judgement and sober spirit for the purpose of prayer. Above all, keep fervent in your love for one another, because love covers a multitude of sins."* Are we living this way? Loving, sober spirit, and sound judgement?

In our world, the choices of men and angel's matter! Can we change the world around us with our prayers? Elijah was bound and determined to see things change! I think to myself, "When would I have called it quits on that mountain?" First time, second time, third time, fourth, fifth, sixth, SEVENTH time? Elijah didn't let the evidence discourage him from fervent prayer. Do we?

If we read on in **James 5:17-18**, we see that James tells us we are people with the same nature as Elijah. *"He prayed earnestly, and the water dried up for three and a half years and then he prayed earnestly, and the heavens opened up and poured water and the earth produced fruit again!"* We have the ability to pray earnestly, and we need to start an understanding of what awesome power that is!!

The choice is yours: Keep praying your "slip and fall Casper milk toast" prayers or settle into a mindset that God does hear you and wants to work His miracles in your life and the lives of others around you and start praying with real purpose!

A few years ago, I was involved in starting up a church in the richest part of Reno. It was a huge undertaking with some really faithful and talented people. We had a Shepherd team of three married couples, all future pastors, and their incredible wives. There was another layman like me, and he and I were both single—me recently divorced after a 24-year marriage, and the other guy in his late 30s never married.

We prayed like crazy people for this endeavor. We prayed at all four corners of the territory of that church plant. We had no building, no members, very little money, no worship team, no one to serve the people and make it run, but we had a Holy mission and a faithful lead pastor, Ryan Griffin, who had the spirit of Elijah.

We met every month for a year and prayer was always the main focus to our mission. There were many times when we prayed, and a strong wind would come out of nowhere and envelope our prayers! God was on our side, and we confessed our sins to each other and put it all in His hands.

One by one the barriers started to fall, and when we opened it in a high school that first Sunday, we were SHOCKED when 500 people walked through the doors! A true blessing considering Reno, Nevada is the second most unchurched city in the country behind San Francisco!

The church grew and grew, and we all served in many ways to fill the gaps. I was asked to lead the prayer team which I took very seriously and assembled a small team of extremely faithful and unselfish people to show up early every Sunday and pray God's blessing on that day. They would be available to pray for every need the church had, or any of its members or visitors had during the week as well. In other words, these people put the priority of corporate prayer for the church and its body even ahead of any personal prayer! What an education that season was for my life on the subject of prayer.

God has continued to grow that church and its body through the hard work and faithfulness of everyone involved. Simply put, our prayers were answered because we were on a mission for God, not our own!

Today I have moved on, but the examples of answered prayer, which are way too many to list, have made a lasting impression on my spirit. I will never doubt the power of God to work in our lives if we wage real prayer and what we are praying for is aligned with His will. And the kicker of all kickers is… the faith we pray with!

LET'S PRAY...

Heavenly Father, all of us need to understand the fact that nothing makes You happier than to be able to answer our prayers. You are a loving Father and want to reward Your children with many Holy blessings. It is so evident that we hamstring our daily prayers with being obsessed with the mortal things of this world. Please change our hearts to align with Your dreams, Father. We need to be active in the lives of others, giving away our hearts in love to help the ones hurting and confused around us. We need to understand that we are just like Elijah and possess the ability to pray with the same urgency. We need to kill off the selfish request we have that Satan fills our hearts with and settle down into a grateful mindset that whatever You do for us is sufficient for the day. I thank You, Lord for these incredible questions we ask ourselves in this chapter. I know that all of us can do a better job of praying for Your will in our lives and helping us to be effective in doing eternal things in the lives of other as well. Morning, noon, and night, Lord! We are Yours. In Christ precious and marvelous Name. **AMEN**

CHAPTER TWENTY-FIVE

Prayer Answered

What is the right response when God answers prayers?

Have you ever been asking for something so long and in such a desperate way that you finally just give up and surrender? What happens to our hearts in that situation is important to understand. I know this from many events in my life, both as a teenager thrown into the big world because of divorce of my parents, and also as an adult who has lived on both sides of the spiritual world and been in so many life and death situations that, if the truth be known, I should have been writing this from behind prison bars... if I was even still alive.

First off, in those defining moments in our lives when we get to the place of surrender, we will find out it's like being on the edge of a steep cliff. We nervously creep up to the edge and look below. Fear grips our hearts as we look down and contemplate the fall. How bad could it hurt? Will we be judged for intentionally going over the edge or should we stage an accidental slip? Yes, that's it! It will be easier to fake a slip going over the side and face the light-speed end to all our broken dreams and hearts. God obviously doesn't care. He is not listening to us, and we are sick of begging, so metaphorically, we're jumping off the cliff in our prayer life and giving up.

Like I've said over and over, our life is a sum of all the choices that we've made toward God and surrender is not a bad choice unless we're doing it with a black heart. The cliff option can manifest itself in so many ways as we struggle to control the outcome by taking every possible, miserable detour available beside surrender. Afterall, we are created with the ability to choose… and that free will separates us from the rest of God's creations.

The choice to surrender is lined with a harsh reality that one way we go off the cliff and quit, or the other way, we turn around and look at the daunting path that leads up to a switch-back trail and straight up the path of another cliff! What a choice! That path is always the harder of the two choices. The cliff seems the easier, and sadly many who get to that desperate, spiritual place chooses the easy way out. But in reality, that cliff is the harder of the two choices because it ultimately means we go it alone. Jump or climb?

The jump has its fatal attraction of finality. "I can't deal with this anymore." This is the surrender of the hopes and plans that once were a battle cry of a young person after life's many mean turns have beat them down to a place of desperate surrender. It's a bad choice that leads back into a mindset of self-destruction, anger, and a life of constant question of God's unfulfilled purpose for our life.

The other choice is to turn around and start to climb again, up the hard straight-up path which is much more challenging and requires an understanding that God is always with us, and we are never alone. It leads us to an understanding that He always answers our prayers in one of three ways. Even when the answer is "No", He is still at work in marvelous ways that will develop us into the person He desires in order to accomplish what He has set out for our life... even if it doesn't look anything like we think it should. The battle cry of the wounded is to pick up our Spiritual weapons and get back in the fight!

The three ways God answers our prayers are:

1. Yes! **2.** No! **3.** I got something better for you!

Part of the problem when we pray is that we always expect and want a yes, because we are programmed from the start to want success in everything! Why is that? Because we are, in a lot of ways, like spoiled brats. First, we pray. Then maybe when things don't go our way, we try and make deals with God. And if that fails, we take matters into our own hands, and we fight and scratch out our way, and take liberties with the people around us, manipulate, steal, or even kill and destroy those in our way. That is the way of the world. The common denominator in all of that is our approach to life with the wrong motivations. Why? Because real men and women take care of business, but in doing things this way, we are profaning God!

Let's look at what the Scriptures say about prayer motivations. In **Ephesians 1:11-13** it says, *"In Him also we have obtained an inheritance, having been predestined according to His purpose who works all things after the council of His will, to the need that we who were the first to hope in Christ would be to the praise of His glory. In Him, you also, after listening to the message of truth, the gospel of your salvation—having also believed, you were sealed in Him with the Holy Spirit of promise."* Where is prayer mentioned here? The answer is that it is not. However, if we truly understand our place in God's heart and our position in His family, then we wouldn't profane Him in our prayers!

So, when we get a "Yes" from Him, it's not some magical, mystical cosmic event. It's simply the fact that we've aligned our prayers with His will for our life! He rewards our faith because we've trusted Him no matter what the outcome! So, what should our response be when we get a "Yes"?

1. Be grateful...eyes up.

2. Be humble...head down.

3. Don't mess it up...don't over think it.

4. Don't try and control it.

5. Keep a pure heart.

Mathew 5:8 says, *"Blessed are the pure of heart, for they shall see God."* Keeping a pure heart is key to making the best out of all our answered prayers! When we are constantly in a mindset of confession and willful obedience, our ability to understand God's plan in our answered prayers will greatly increase. This fact is so paramount to keep us from over thinking our good fortune and acting on our mission that He has given us by granting our prayers.

So, what should we do when we get a "No" answer to our prayers? How should we react? Should we kick and scream and be miserable? Should we pout and turn in on our Christian walk, or get bitter in Spirit and poison our hearts and the lives of those around us? No! The right response to a "No" from God is:

1. Be grateful...eyes up.

2. Be humble...head down.

3. Don't mess it up...don't over think it.

4. Don't try and control it.

5. Look at your motives.

6. Keep a pure heart.

James 4:3 says, *"You ask and do not receive, because you ask with wrong motives, so that you may spend it on your pleasures."* Our motives are always suspect if we're being completely honest! When we pray, we need to get into a mindset of discipline to check our motives. Are we praying for this thing for any selfish reason? Is the reason that God is giving us a "No" because of that? How do we change our hearts to a pure heart and accept the "No" in a positive constructive way? By striving to keep a pure heart we are responding to life's ups and downs like a Godly person. **Proverbs 16:2** says, *"All the ways of a man are clean in his own sight, but the Lord weighs the motives."*

So, what should we do if we get, "I got something better for you." Or, in other words, that we all seem to hate in our ballistic world is, "WAIT"!

1. Be grateful… eyes up.
2. Be humble… heads down.
3. Learn to wait without complaint.
4. Trust Him… don't try to control it.
5. Look for ways to improve your walk.

Maybe there are areas of your life that just don't measure up, and He is going to work with you and help you make those critical changes for your own good before He just dishes out a bunch of "Yes" answers! Are you making a real effort to keep His commandments? Do you even know what those commandments are? Can you repeat the Ten Commandments from memory? I bet 90% of the Christians walking the earth today cannot.

Are you protecting your lifestyle or constantly flirting with the dark side on secret things, secret lustful thoughts? Are you going invisible and committing secret sins that you wrongly think you're getting away with? **1 John 3:21-22** says, *"Beloved, if our heart does not condemn us, we have confidence before God; and whatever we ask we receive from Him, because we keep His commandments and do the things that are pleasing in His sight."*

So here is the million-dollar question: Are the things you are doing in your life pleasing in His sight? Only you can answer this, and only you can begin to change the things that are not pleasing in His sight! God stands ready to walk alongside you and empower you with the help of the Holy Spirit, **if** you let Him.

We always have choices and the end game, the wrap-up of our

lives, is going to be on the big screen someday for all the souls to see. It is in the end a question of, did you accept Jesus as your Lord and Savior? Did you confess your sins and acknowledge His sacrifice on the cross? And, even though this next part won't affect your salvation, did you move in this world obeying His commandments and forgiving and showing grace and love to as many as you could?

Yes. No. I've got something better for you! What do all three answers have in common?

1. Be grateful... eyes up
2. Be humble... head down
3. Don't try to control it... stay in the game

LET'S PRAY...

Dear Heavenly Father, who lives and breathes all life abundantly everywhere at all times forever, let us thank You now for never turning a deaf ear to our prayers. You always know in Your infinite wisdom what is best for us, and when to move the circumstances of our life so that it will direct us to seek You in a more deep and meaningful way. You have so much love and grace for us and all we need to do is humble ourselves, obey Your Word and follow the direction of the Holy Spirit that You have gifted us with. We ask forgiveness for our human shortcomings and how it plays out in our thoughts, words, and deeds. We ask that You give us the ability to move in this time and place to share the love You have bestowed on us, and to help the people around us find You in the same way we have. Help us to be grateful Lord, help us to be humble Lord, and don't take us out of the game! We all want to be first-string starters who play both ways and never come out until our time here is over, Lord and we come to be with You in glory for eternity. We ask all these things in the Mighty Name of Your Son, and our Royal Priest Savior, Jesus Christ! **AMEN**

CHAPTER TWENTY-SIX

When All is Said and Done

There is no such thing as unanswered prayer! God is always working on our behalf if we are seeking His direction in our lives. Despite our human limitations to understand this and accept it, He never stops, even when we are completely disrespectful and disobedient towards Him. I believe we act like children who are mad at our parents and act out in defiance thinking we are punishing them, when in reality, the consequences of our actions will squarely fall upon our own shoulders eventually.

If you're acting this way toward your Heavenly Father, tell me, "How's it working out for you?" There is an agonizing black cloud over your spirit that never seems to go away and nothing you do in this world seems to fix it. He is watching you with a graceful eye and tweaking the events and the people you meet to bring you back to Him when you reach your breaking point.

If you love Him and have accepted Jesus as your Savior, but you still haven't gone all in, He is watching you, and He's waiting for the right time to affect you in such a way, that nothing this world has that you're hanging onto will matter to you. He is waiting anxiously for your heart to change and to seek His will, instead of yours, in all things that are you!

If you're moving around this life with a constant drizzle of a cloud that never stops dripping over you, and every now and then you see a glimpse of the sunshine, but you never fully get warm in it, maybe you're not in the ominous black cloud thunderstorm, but just a constant drizzle of rain that reminds you something must be wrong.

As you grow spiritually in this crazy way of life, you begin to understand with certain clarity that God is always on your side, and that there is a bigger picture going on around you that the human condition and our ability to act in free will never totally understand. You learn to live by faith, believing in what cannot always be seen or that cannot be explained by way of science or our limited flesh and bone logic. You simply cave in gloriously to His will, and there comes over you such a peace. It is a wonderful place to be when you know with absolute certainty that God is always looking out for you.

You pray differently. Your selfish motivations are controlled and confessed. Your expectations of answers are checked with patience, and the fact that you have utter confidence that He knows what the best way is to answer your prayers. And it's enough to keep you going, even if you're tired and weary because you believe with every cell in your body that there is no such thing as unanswered prayer.

So, get comfortable with talking to Him; laugh at the tough times with Him; enjoy His sense of humor. Keep Him close all day, not just for an hour or two on Sunday; be generous with the poor; and take an active role in helping those in need around you; get involved in a Church community and don't just take from them, but give of yourself and your story. Share your struggles, pray with them, and share grace and love.

You need to realize that there is a very real spiritual war going on in this world between good and evil, and don't be naïve to the fact that once you change teams and get on the winning side, you're going to become a big target for the enemy! Pray for protection **at all times**, memorize scripture and read your Bible as much as you can. Pray for protection for your lifestyle and those you run with. Assimilating into bad company will always get you into hard times. Pray for help in beating the secret sins you flirt with because everything you do, think, or say is always before God's eyes. There is never a time when you go invisible despite how crafty you plan your secret sin.

THE SUCCESS OF YOUR LIFE HERE ON THIS EARTH IS DETERMINED BY THE SUM TOTAL OF ALL THE DECISIONS YOU MAKE TOWARD GOD, and what He has planned for you. Thankfully we serve a merciful God, who forgives our bad decisions and restores us to good standing when we ask with pure hearts. Why try and go this rocky uphill path alone? He wants us to talk to Him in prayer. He wants to help us make good decisions. He has work for us to do, and He wants us to get about it! We are His warriors. To quote a true modern-day warrior, Jocko Willink, "Get Some".

My prayer for you is that the perspective of this book on prayer will help you rethink the traditional misconceptions of prayer and start you on a rich and rewarding and open dialog with God who has been waiting for you to open communication with Him since the day you were conceived. This thing we do is a "heart thing" and it cannot be faked. God looks at your heart as you express your prayers.

May God bless you and the ones you love in mighty ways, and may He use you to multiple His Kingdom and His glory! **AMEN**

CHAPTER TWENTY-SEVEN

On My Knees

Just In Case

LET'S PRAY AGAIN...

Father God, we are powerless over Satan and evil. We know and understand without Your protection we have no authority over the forces of evil, so we ask in the most serious and sincere way that You protect us from evil, that You give us the kind of hearts and purpose to face the dark side with a complete confidence that comes from being one of Your powerful children. We ask for courage to get back out into the battles of this life empowered by the Holy Spirit to do Your work and affect the lives of our lost friends and relatives. We ask for the boldness to pray with hurting strangers on the streets of our towns. We ask for the guts to speak out at our jobs and for the power to live Godly lives and not bring shame to Your causes. Give us this amazing work to do Lord. Help us to seek peace with everyone and to be instruments of love, not hate and bitterness. Change our hearts to be peacemakers and forgive the ones who hurt us and to love our current enemies! We know Satan is real and he commands the evil forces at work here, but we seek to be used by You, Lord, to counter his evil plans and move our brothers and sisters to a safe camp at Your feet! Help us to be real warriors, not tasteless salt hiding in Your churches and just waiting for You to fix it all. In the name of Jesus Christ our Lord. **AMEN**

LET'S PRAY AGAIN...

Father in Heaven, forgive me for my sin. Give me Your grace and grant me unmerited favor because I do not deserve it. I believe Your Son came to this earth for the one purpose. And that was to live a perfect life in human flesh, be tempted in all the ways we are tempted, and yet without sin. As we give our lives to Him in thankfulness, Father. Protect my heart from making the same mistake over and over. Give me the sound judgement to forgive those who have hurt me and forgive those who plan evil against me. You control all things in my life, and You are always faithful to give me the strength to trust You in all things, even to learn how to forgive endlessly because that is the meaning of 7x70! Forgive me, Lord, as I have forgiven those who have hurt me! Hear my prayers, Father, because I ask these things according to Your will, not mine. And I ask them in the Mighty Name of Jesus Christ, Your Son and My Savior! **AMEN**

LET'S PRAY AGAIN...

Lord God, Master of all things. We ask You in total faith, without a sliver of doubt, to give us wisdom and to let us in on the big picture of life. Give us the strength to trust our lessons that You allow us to make. Those lessons that help draw us closer to You. And give us a fire that will allow us to make it through as stronger, more mature Christians… braver and fearless as the challenges in the world come at us. Give us eyes and hearts to be bold to the lost and hurting people around us who suffer from the same things we have been through. Give us hearts to care for ourselves. In Jesus' Mighty Name and Power, we ask for a natural reaction of turning to prayer and trusting in You in adversity. **AMEN**

LET'S PRAY AGAIN…

Dear Jesus, our true Commander and Chief, please cause us to realize how very important we all are to the war You have called us to in the souls of humanity. What an honor to serve such a righteous cause. Give us a raw dose of courage, strengthen our resolve to serve with pure hearts, unselfish motives and to love our worthy enemies. Thank You, Lord that You recruited us, You train us, You discipline us when necessary and You launch us into battle, but never alone. You are with our every step in the front as the point man. You are in command and all we need to do is obey. The victory is guaranteed! Our service is truly a heart thing! Protect us as we serve, in Your Son's precious and Holy name, Jesus Christ. **AMEN**

LET'S PRAY AGAIN…

Dear Heavenly Father of all life, I humbly come before You on my knees today with a heavy heart and a desire to repair the areas of my life that drive me into a place where I do not value myself like You value me. I ask You to help me answer these questions. Show me what I need to see about myself and how I got this way. Please, Lord, keep me from avoiding the truth. Help me see my inner fears on a daily basis and help me surrender them to You. Teach me what I really need to view myself correctly and then use me, Lord, in any way You see fit. Holy Spirit, rise up in me and show me the way to confidence and grace. Show me, Father, when I am being self-abusive and help me put that behind me so I can be more like Your Son who You sent to die on a cross for me. And it is in His Name, Jesus Christ, that I pray. **AMEN**

LET'S PRAY AGAIN...

My Lord of all strength and mercy, what an area of growth You have set before us and what a wonderful reality it is that You set Your angels around us from falling too far from You. You expect us to do our part in controlling our desires and not turning them into evil actions. A true challenge we are capable of **if** we use the power of the Holy Spirit and fling our hearts into action as soon as we start off the deep end. Give us the strength, Lord, to take this incredible human challenge seriously and to gain wisdom and foresight into the bad life results that will come when we lose self-control. It never ends good. Give us a desire to equip ourselves with weapons of the Spirit and the courage to fight the most important battles we face... the ones within us. In Your Son's Precious and Holy Name. **AMEN**

LET'S PRAY AGAIN...

God above all things, Creator of all things, hear our prayer for help this day. Help the ones who love You to have the courage to be happy in whatever situation, whatever station in life on this earth You have us in with a glad heart. We have so much in this life we take for granted and so many blessings around us that at times we grow blind to the blessings You have given us and focus on the wrong things. Lord, give us wisdom to be a future-focused Christian. Help us to learn to suffer without complaint in the world. Help us to grasp that You may have a better plan for us than we are planning, and that we will be so much better off trusting in Your timing. Forgive our dissatisfaction and strengthen our hearts to be a rock of faith and a witness to all who know us, that You are our God, and we trust You in every single little thing in our life. Hear this prayer, Lord. How can it not be Your will? Grant us the requests we ask, Lord. Protect us from the evil one and his evil army. Help us to mount up with wings of eagles, Lord and live a life with a happy heart worthy of Your sacrifice on the cross. In Jesus' Holy and Precious Name. **AMEN**

LET'S PRAY AGAIN...

Dear Father of Peace, help us to have a mindset of peace. Help us to keep our focus on the mission field around us that we can affect by showing grace and peace to everyone around us. Help us forgive with pure hearts and mend relationships with friends and family. Help us to be neutral to the conflicts in this world and in our country so that we may be instruments of peace and not fan the flame of hate that Satan is stoking now in our world. Please, God, give us confidence that no matter what rocks are flying our way, the pain of the blows will be nothing compared to the glory we will see someday when we sit at your feet and know true eternal peace. When the lion and the lamb will sit next to each other, and no fear will be present. Help us to be solid in our purpose and realize that true peace lies within our hearts and not in the world around us. In Christ Holy name, I pray. **AMEN**